Becoming a Woman
After God's Own Heart

Encouragement for Christian Moms

Written by
ANGELA LEIFELD

Copyright © 2016 by Angela Leifeld

Becoming a Woman After God's Own Heart
Encouragement for Christian Moms
by Angela Leifeld

Printed in the United States of America.

Edited by Xulon Press.

ISBN 9781498484725

All rights reserved solely by the author. The author guarantees all contents are original and do not infringe upon the legal rights of any other person or work. No part of this book may be reproduced in any form without the permission of the author. The views expressed in this book are not necessarily those of the publisher.

Unless otherwise indicated, Scripture quotations taken from the New Century Version (NCV). Copyright © 2005 by Thomas Nelson, Inc. Used by permission. All rights reserved.

Scripture quotations taken from the New King James Version (NKJV). Copyright © 1982 by Thomas Nelson, Inc. Used by permission. All rights reserved.

Scripture quotations taken from the English Standard Version (ESV). Copyright © 2001 by Crossway, a publishing ministry of Good News Publishers. Used by permission. All rights reserved.

Scripture quotations taken from the Holy Bible, New International Version (NIV). Copyright © 1973, 1978, 1984, 2011 by Biblica, Inc.™. Used by permission. All rights reserved.

Scripture quotations taken from the Holy Bible, New Living Translation (NLT). Copyright ©1996, 2004, 2007 by Tyndale House Foundation. Used by permission of Tyndale House Publishers, Inc.

Scripture quotations taken from the King James Version (KJV) – *public domain.*

www.xulonpress.com

Dedication

This book is dedicated to the following people:

- To my grandparents, Reverend Ernest and Melva Chambers, who modeled for me what it meant to walk with the Lord all the days of their lives. As a child, hearing my grandfather pray at prayer meetings taught me to speak from my heart whenever talking to God and to ask for God's blessings and guidance for my marriage, my children, and over my life. Their influence to trust the Lord in all things still guides my thoughts and decisions today.

- To my parents, Ken and Wilma Robinson, who taught me to love Jesus from my earliest memories as a child.

- To my children, Cassie, Jerad, Austin, and Justin. My greatest wish for each of you is to love and serve the Lord in your lifetimes.

    Cassie, you are my only daughter. God knew what He was doing when He gave me only one girl. However, I cannot imagine my life as a mother without the experience of raising a girl. You have grown into a beautiful young woman, inside and out.

Jerad, your passion for excellence inspires not only your younger brothers, but also all of those you come in contact with on a daily basis. The closeness of the relationship you have with your dad is incredible and awesome to watch grow as your mom. I will always be grateful for the way you show respect and love to us as your parents.

Austin and Justin, you have taught me to laugh more than I ever thought possible. I will always be grateful that God blessed us with twin boys. I enjoy watching you grow as individuals, but I am also thankful that both of you cherish the bond you have in being a twin.

- To my wonderful and loving husband, Ken. Your love and support for me as your wife are immeasurable. You are my best friend.

This book has been a long time in the writing. I think it is only fitting to dedicate it to the ones who gave me the material I have used to write it.

Contents

Dedication v
Introduction xv
Acknowledgments xi

Chapter One: This is 9-1-1—May I Help You? 17
Chapter Two: Sunday's A'Comin'! 24
Chapter Three: Where Can I Find Real Answers? 29
Chapter Four: A Perfect "10"? 42
Chapter Five: Isn't It Amazing What a Prayer Can Do? 55
Chapter Six: Finding the Calm in the Storm 65
Chapter Seven: What Kind of Love Is This? 77
Chapter Eight: Career or Not a Career—That's the Question! 93
Chapter Nine: G.R.O.W.T.H. 16 106

Endorsements

"This book is a must-read for women struggling to live a God-centered life in the tumult and trauma of today's world. Angela Leifeld's own coming-of-age story and how she seeks to serve God with radical obedience will make you laugh, cry and – mostly – use the grace and wisdom of her words to overcome heart-break and pain, be more loving and devoted leaders, and more passionately serve God."

—Ellen Leifeld,
retired newspaper publisher

"She is real. She is insightful. It is easy to identify with her honesty. Angela has a gift of sharing that helps all of us find hope, like a glass of cold water on a hot and humid day. She weaves in a biblical foundation that provides confidence that her truth is HIS TRUTH. Her voice and laughter rise from the page and speak to the youthful single woman, the new mom, the working weary and the wise grandma. Her wisdom strengthens me so that I can guide and lead others. What a wonderful way to begin or end the day! I hope she never stops writing."

—Renee Hyde
Assistant Superintendent Papillion-LaVista School District

"Angela Leifeld has written a very candid, self-revealing guide for moms seeking to deepen their Christian faith and to better cope with daily trials. Written from the perspective of a loving parent and educator, *Becoming a Woman After God's Own Heart* illuminates a path to greater enthusiasm and trust. It will bolster those seeking clarity and direction from their faith."

—John Baylor
President, John Baylor Prep

Acknowledgments

$\mathcal{I}$ would like to extend a special thanks to the following people who have encouraged me as a Christian, as a wife, as a mom, and as an educator. Each of you has influenced me in my journey. I am grateful that God places people in our lives for a moment, a season, or a lifetime.

Dawn Selleck, thank you for teaching me how to trust God through prayer. Our Sunday evening prayer sessions asking for God's guidance led each of us to follow Him obediently into new adventures.

Karen Palmberg, you are a true inspiration to me as a Christian woman. I would not have survived my first year as a principal without your support, love, and encouragement. I will be forever grateful for the way you cared for my family, especially Cassie and Jerad. Thank you for leading Jerad to Christ as a little boy.

Mary Miller, all of our daily walks and talks about how God was working in our lives has inspired me to be bolder in sharing my faith. I am so grateful that you were not only my neighbor, but that you have become one of my dearest friends.

Lori Ludwig, I thank God that you and I not only got to work together for a season but that we became prayer warriors for our school together. Thank you for believing in me as your principal but more importantly as a sister in Christ.

Cris Noerrlinger, your friendship has been instrumental in my Christian walk. Thank you for agreeing to be an accountability partner! I know that I can call you at any time and you will pray with me at that exact moment.

Dawnelle Martin, I am extremely grateful that God gave us so much in common when I moved to the Beaver Lake area. I will always cherish attending and cheering on our girls during softball, basketball and track together. Your friendship and constant support truly helped me to become a better Christian, mom, wife, and educator.

Conestoga Bible Study Ladies: Cris, Dawnelle, Denise, Carol, Kim, Beth and Monica. Studying God's Word with you ladies was so much fun! I pray for all of you often!

Humphrey Bible Study Ladies: Denise, Pam, Mitzi and Mariam. I am so grateful that God has brought us together to study His Word. I enjoy growing and learning in Christ with you ladies.

George Robertson, thank you for believing in me enough to hire me as the first woman principal in Mead, Nebraska! I will be forever grateful that I had the opportunity to work with you as a fellow educator.

Dan Woods, Bill McCallister, and Mike Cunning, each of you have inspired me as an educator as well as a Christian. Attending Fellowship of Christian Administrators (FCA) and meeting each of you my first year as a principal has helped me to become a better leader. I appreciate your wisdom and guidance over the years.

Candy Becher, thank you for offering to read and edit my first draft of this book. Your words of encouragement helped me to take it to the next step and finally publish it.

Mike Teahon, thank you for encouraging me to write this book. Asking me each year if I had gotten that book published yet kept it in the back of my mind for years.

Acknowledgments

Renee Hyde, I cannot begin to express how wonderful it is to have you as a friend and fellow administrator. Your patience and focus as an educational leader, mom, and grandma inspires me.

A special thank you to Megan Danner for designing the cover of my first book. I described what I was thinking and she brought my vision to life.

Introduction

As I sat down to seriously consider writing this book, once again dinner boiled over on the stove. Yes, I can cook. However, I usually seem to be running from place to place, so food isn't my highest priority. It's more of a luxury for my family to have a home-cooked meal. Some families look forward to eating out, but my family gets excited when Mom makes a real, home-cooked meal, not Hamburger Helper or mac and cheese.

So here is where I began: during my break from school and in the midst of running to baseball and softball games, summer league basketball, camps of every sort, and potty-training two little boys— yes, I said *two*. More importantly, I was trying to listen for God's voice in the noise of the world and desperately wanted to serve Christ in the mission He had selected instead of with my own agenda.

God had been showing me a need, and it was huge. I finally realized that there are many Christian mothers who are also career moms stretched beyond their own strength, trying to live the best examples they know how for their children. As moms, we are so busy taking care of our families; we neglect ourselves not only physically but also spiritually. We have to be supermoms, and whom do we dare speak to about our feelings of inadequacy without sounding *weak*?

Whether you are a full-time stay-at-home mom (God bless each one of you—I could not do it!) or a career mom, we face the same battles. There simply is not enough time for ourselves. I hope this book will encourage you, strengthen you, and remind you that God is always within reach. He doesn't mind answering our 9-1-1 calls, but He truly wants a close and personal walk with each of us. He wants our joys, our sorrows, our worries, and most importantly, He wants our hearts.

Chapter One

This Is 9-1-1—May I Help You?

"This is 9-1-1—may I help you?"

I looked up from my Bible and stared at the twins' riding toy in the dark living room corner. *Wow! That was strange,* I thought to myself.

It was 5:00 a.m. on March 14, 2005. I knew I was the only one awake in my family. I turned back to my Bible and devotional and started to silently read again.

"This is 9-1-1—may I help you?"

There it went again. Now I started to think that I was losing my mind, because that toy was not supposed to play unless you pushed a button. A strange feeling came over me, like someone was watching me. I tried to shake the eeriness and concentrate harder on my open Bible. I was determined to read what I needed for the day, and I was not going to be distracted from my task— not by a child's riding toy, anyway.

About fifteen minutes later, the toy spoke again: "This is 9-1-1—may I help you?" Okay, this was really weird, and the hair on the back of my neck stood up. It was completely black outside, and the only light on was the light above my desk in the kitchen.

"Lord," I prayed, *"if You are trying to get my attention and I'm not getting it, please tell me. I am—"*

"This is 9-1-1—may I help you?"

"This is 9-1-1—may I help you?"

"This is 9-1-1—may I help you?"

The toy spoke three times in a row without taking a break.

I prayed humbly, *"Father, You have my attention. What is it I am missing? Help me listen and hear Your voice."*

"I wait for the LORD, my soul waits, and in his word I hope; my soul waits for the LORD more than watchmen wait for the morning, more than watchmen wait for the morning" (Psalm 130:5–6 ESV). Suddenly these verses took on new meaning for me. What if I had lived during biblical times and was a night watchman? My job would have been to walk the brick walls of the city, to peer carefully into utter darkness while trying to protect the city all night long, *without* electricity. Today, even when I have a light on, the shadows of the darkness still make me a bit skittish.

Think about it. The night sky would be completely black on cloudy nights, and on clear nights the stars and moon might yield a little bit of light to aid me in my job. I am not sure this would be a job I would enjoy too much.

Today we have electricity readily available in the United States. Even on the darkest nights, we can still see lights in the distance from yards, barns, streets, and even entire towns. It is never completely black.

Can you imagine an ad for a night watchman in biblical times?

HELP WANTED: NIGHT WATCHMAN

Duties for position:
- Protect the city from all intruders.
- Keen eyesight required.

- Lighted torch available, but you must always have your own sword and trumpet handy to warn the city of danger.

The anticipation for the morning would be great, I would think. You would know that danger could be lurking in the shadows, and at any given moment, your own life could be in danger. I would be watching for any hint of the sunrise, and it would bring relief when the sky began to lighten, especially on the blackest nights.

"My soul waits for the LORD more than watchmen wait for the morning, more than watchmen wait for the morning" (Psalm 130:6 ESV). Waiting for the Lord more than watchmen wait for the morning means anticipating God's presence and guidance more than longing for the sunrise after a fearful night of work. It means putting our hope and complete trust in the Lord. He wants us to wait patiently for His answers. God commands us to wait eagerly for guidance, help, and courage.

In Hosea 6:3, the Bible says, "Let's try to learn about the LORD; he will come to us as surely as the dawn comes. He will come to us like rain, like the spring rain that waters the ground."

I have never been very fond of the dark. Now that my husband and I have four children, if I want time alone with God to read, study, and pray, it has to be in the wee hours of the morning. This means it is usually still dark, especially in the winter. The quietness of the morning and the single light I use for reading remind me of several promises. God is my light in the darkness, my provider, my protector, my healer, and my shepherd.

Back to the toy repeating, "This is 911—may I help you?" It didn't play again after I asked God if He was speaking to me. As I finished my devotions and started getting ready to wake my children and meet the troops at school, I still was a bit puzzled by the experience with a speaking toy.

I prayed to myself, *"Lord, there must be more You want me to hear or see, because using a child's toy is pretty unusual."*

I dropped Jerad, a fifth-grader, off at school, and the twins, Austin and Justin, at day care. I then took Cassie to the high school for swing choir practice. As I continued my seven-mile drive to the middle school, I shut off the radio and again asked God to explain about the toy. I told Him He had my attention and I was going nuts with curiosity. *"Please, Lord,"* I prayed, *"let me hear You and understand the message."*

A small still voice inside of me said, *This is a chapter title of the book you are going to write.*

What! Me . . . a writer? I thought, somewhat panic-stricken. "Lord, I know You told me You want me to start speaking to women, but write a book? And besides, who would want to hear about my crazy life?"

Angie, this is the first chapter of your first book.

My mind was racing faster than I usually drive. Those of you who have had the opportunity to ride with me can only imagine the speed of my brain at that moment. This was the second time that I had heard God tell me He had a mission for me and that writing a book was part of it. The thought of writing an entire book and having people read it scared me a little bit. Okay, it scared me a lot!

What if people don't like it? Where am I going to find the time as well as the material to write a book? Can I really do this, Lord? I silently asked.

The truth of the matter is God doesn't care what other people think. He wants our complete obedience. And why was I asking about my own abilities? Doesn't my strength come from Him?

"So know that the LORD your God is God, the faithful God. He will keep his agreement of love for a thousand lifetimes for people who love him and obey his commands" (Deuteronomy 7:9). A thousand lifetimes is unfathomable to me, and obviously absolute obedience is a necessity.

In 1 Samuel 15, the Lord rejected Saul as king because of his disobedience. God gave specific instructions through Samuel for Saul to go to war and to destroy everything that belonged to the Amalekites. In fact, God specifically told Samuel to give these words to Saul: "Now go, attack the Amalekites and totally destroy all that belongs to them. Do not spare them; put to death men and women, children and infants, cattle and sheep, camels and donkeys" (verse 3).

Saul's army was unwilling to destroy King Agag and the best of the sheep and cattle. However, since Saul was victorious, he thought that he had been obedient to God's commands. When questioned by Samuel about his disobedience, Saul excused his actions by explaining that he kept the best sheep and cattle to sacrifice to the Lord.

"But Samuel replied, 'Does the Lord delight in burnt offerings and sacrifices as much as in obeying the Lord? To obey is better than sacrifice, and to heed is better than the fat of rams'" (1 Samuel 15:22 NIV).

This one act of disobedience cost King Saul God's favor forever. God requires complete obedience. He expects us to conform to His will and to complete the mission He has assigned to us.

It was obvious to me that God wanted my commitment to this project. I was intrigued by the idea of writing a book but also wondered if God was talking to the right person. I am not usually one to back down from a challenge; however, in my eyes, this sounded like climbing Mount Everest without oxygen.

In fact, my desire to always be the best, to be perfect, and to please everyone has had its ups and downs. One of my best friends once said to me, "Angie, God made us human beings, not human doings! You need to learn to say no once in a while." Unfortunately, God has had to not only slow me down at times, but also bring me to a complete halt on numerous occasions to get my attention.

God wants us to find time just to be with Him. It has taken me several years to figure this out. However, since I have made a conscious effort to start each day alone in the presence of God, He has revealed so many things to me. I have become more aware of His voice and His leading in all daily matters.

In John 10:4–5, Jesus states, "When he has brought out all his own, he goes on ahead of them, and his sheep follow him because they know his voice. But they will never follow a stranger; in fact, they will run away from him because they do not recognize a stranger's voice" (NIV). If we spend time listening to our Master, we will recognize His voice even in the noisiest places. We will follow Jesus in the darkness. We don't need to see Him, because we can hear Him calling.

Faith is a state of mind that grows out of our actions, so obedience is the key to *real* faith. Obedience does not just know what's right, but acts upon what is right—not just belief, but belief lived out. We must know the voice of God so we can act upon it. Our faith grows as we surrender more of ourselves to act in obedience to the Word.

Two days later, I shared my crazy encounter with the riding toy and God's message with a very dear friend. During the conversation, I realized that I had been writing material for a book for years. I had started sending a verse and words of encouragement to two friends each day on e-mail almost seven years ago. The endeavor started after Dawn's son was hit and killed by a car and Karen had to move to California because of the health of her husband. Karen's husband had been my pastor, and he had to step down from the pulpit because of unforeseen complications as a result of a surgery.

Soon after, word spread. Before long I was sending the devotional e-mails to about 130 people, and today that audience is much broader because I also post the devotionals on Facebook. Posting my devotionals on Facebook in the beginning was something I struggled with, but in the end I felt like I was being called to be more public with my faith. It was yet a new way to act on my obedience to God. I have been overwhelmed by the number of people, young and old, embracing God's message through Facebook.

Guess what? I enjoy doing this! I also love receiving e-mail and Facebook messages saying that my words of encouragement (the Holy Spirit speaking through my typing) has somehow touched someone, made them think about their own relationship with Christ, or was just what they needed to pull through a tough day.

I realized, I could do this. I loved sharing God's goodness and His provision for my daily needs. I enjoyed writing and glorifying God.

Folks, we all need to be faithful in using our talents to glorify and honor God. God says in Numbers 14:24, "But my servant Caleb thinks differently and follows me completely. So I will bring him into the land he has already seen, and his children will own that land."

Jesus says, "Give, and you will receive. You will be given much. Pressed down, shaken together, and running over, it will spill into your lap. The way you give to others is the way God will give to you" (Luke 6:38). We can never out-give God.

So God's "This is 9-1-1—may I help you?" call to me on that early morning of March 14, 2005, has actually turned into a way for me to be a more effective ambassador for Christ.

Chapter Two

Sunday's A'Comin'!

Some days it feels that we are living in such troubling times. Daily we are bombarded with news of bullies, murderers, drug abuse, and terrorism, and it seems that everyone is pointing the finger at someone else. Plus, with the general conversations about how children seem to have no morals, it can be disheartening as well as discouraging for almost anyone.

This happened to be another tough week for society. The front-page story was about a high school student in Minnesota who killed several people in his school and then turned the gun on himself. This young man was bullied and also had disturbing behaviors including obsession with neo-Nazism. Among his belongings were found disturbing pictures that he drew of satanic-like creatures.

Because I am a school administrator, these types of stories really hit home. This had been a particularly long week disciplining students for bullying. I said to myself, *Lord, the task is too great. How can I possibly make a difference?*

Thankfully, the Lord sent His answer of encouragement. It was a message from Psalm 121. It begins, "I look up to the hills, but where does my help come from?" Later in the same psalm, David goes on to say,

"The Lord will protect you from all dangers; he will guard your life. The Lord will guard you as you come and go, both now and forever" (Psalm 121:1, 7–8).

On this particular Tuesday as I left school, the only thought I had when it was finally time to rush and pick up the twins at day care was a breath prayer: "Lord, thank You for keeping me mentally tough today." This was one of those days I would not have survived without looking to the hills for guidance in the morning; God's strength had carried me.

The day before, I had attended a funeral for our superintendent's brother-in-law, who was only forty-two years old and killed in an accident. From the awesome stories told by friends and family, it was obvious that he was well thought of and loved deeply. Doug had been a biker. Many people who were there did not appear to be people who attended a church service on a regular basis. Not only did the pastor share some comforting memories about this man, but he also used this opportunity to give an awesome sermon inviting people to find comfort not only from their wonderful memories, but also by seeking Jesus and a relationship with the Father.

Guess what psalm he used for comfort? You guessed it, Psalm 121. I realized, sitting in the funeral home, that many of these people needed Jesus. I found myself prompted by the Holy Spirit to diligently pray for any lost soul hearing the pastor's words to seek the true answer and meaning to life. I also prayed for the family and friends in attendance who knew the Lord but needed strength and comfort to face losing a beloved son, a brother, an uncle, or a close friend.

In times of sorrow, it can be so hard to understand tragedy or why God has taken away a loved one. In our grief, we have difficulty seeing the big picture. In Psalm 139:16, we are told, "You saw my body as it was formed. All the days planned for me were written in your book before I was one day old." God knew *before* the day of each person's birth that they would be at *this* funeral at this time. He knew that some people needed a wake-up call to serve God more obediently. He knew that the faith of Doug's family members would be an example to those around them to seek the Lord's goodness and mercy. Most importantly, God used this death to have people hear an invitation to find Jesus.

You may be asking which week of the year brought such profound insight. This particularly troublesome week was Easter week in 2005. For years, as an educator and especially as an administrator, I have often pondered, "Why does March always seem to be such a terrible month at school?" In the past, I chalked up the increased craziness and need for discipline to several factors that seemed reasonable to me:

1. It had been a long winter.
2. The students had not been able to be outside and get fresh air.
3. It had been a while since we had Christmas break.
4. Third quarter was ending, and most students, especially seniors, were counting down to the end of the school year.
5. My tolerance for "stupid" actions was at its all-time lowest.

This year, after discussing the events of the week with a very close friend and mentor of mine, I finally realized that evil rears its ugly head during the Lenten season *each* year. The significance of March doesn't really have anything to do with the calendar year; it has everything to do with the season we are preparing to celebrate.

We are getting ready to celebrate Easter Sunday, the day of resurrection which has significance for all Christians. We are celebrating the most important day of the year, the day Jesus Christ freed us from sin and gave us the opportunity for eternal life in heaven. We are singing praises for

Christ's victory over death and for those who have been released from the hold of Satan.

Satan lost the battle so many years ago. He thought he was destroying God's plan to save mankind, but instead he enabled Jesus' death and resurrection to happen by planting the idea of betrayal into Judas Iscariot's heart. Each year we celebrate God's gift through the sacrifice of His Son. And each year, I am sure, Satan doesn't enjoy Christians rejoicing in his defeat and Christ's victory.

Do not be disheartened when Satan comes to discourage you. Keep in mind he doesn't want joyous Christians sharing the good news. He wants us down and out so we will be too tired to celebrate and too defeated to further God's kingdom. I want to share a couple of thoughts that have kept me encouraged during some difficult times in the past:

> If I weren't making a difference for God's kingdom, Satan wouldn't feel the need to bother me.

> And my favorite comforting thought: If Satan is picking on me, maybe he is leaving some of my fellow brothers and sisters in Christ alone.

Isaiah 43:2 says, "When you pass through the waters, I will be with you. When you cross the rivers, you will not drown. When you walk through fire, you will not be burned, nor will the flames hurt you." This verse is God's assurance of His constant presence. God promises to protect and guide us. He is with us wherever we go all of the time. However, we may need to cross some raging waters or walk through some fire to strengthen our faith.

There are times that the seasons of our lives seem too difficult. Can you imagine the agony Jesus felt on the night He was betrayed? He had walked with these twelve men for three years. He knew the disciples were going to run and hide. Not only did Jesus know what was going to happen on Friday, but He also knew He was going to have to face it alone. He knew what He was going to have to endure for our sins, yet He told His Father, "Not My will, but Yours be done."

I am thankful that God doesn't always tell me what is going to happen next. I am thankful that I know God will be with me in all circumstances, especially difficult situations. I am thankful that we are promised not only that temptations will come, but also that they are common to all men. Bust most importantly, God will always provide a way out (1 Corinthians 10:13).

So just remember, it may seem like Friday, but Sunday's a'comin'!

Chapter Three

Where Can I Find Real Answers?

When I look back and ponder the difficulties and trials I have faced, I am constantly amazed at the lessons learned and at God's timing to reveal the reasons for heartache or blessing. I have begged God for answers as to why He would allow something to happen, and God plainly said, "Angie, wait! You cannot understand right now. Wait on Me."

I hate waiting. I don't like slow drivers (my many speeding tickets vouch for my hurry-up attitude on the road). It is really hard for me when people drag their feet on making decisions, especially if there really isn't another way of doing it. Plus, it makes me completely crazy when people wait until the last minute to make plans.

I am the first to admit that patience is an area of opportunity that God has used to teach me valuable lessons in the last several years. When I feel like things are not going the way I think they should, I am reminded that God is always in control. Now, I humbly pray, "You are in control, and I trust You. Forgive me for trying to do this on my own."

First Peter 5:7–9 says, "Casting all your care upon Him, for He cares for you. Be sober, be vigilant; because your adversary the devil walks about like a roaring lion, seeking whom he may devour. Resist him, steadfast in the faith, knowing that the same sufferings are experienced by your brotherhood in the world" (NKJV).

Worrying is useless. Thoughts of doubt and worry are not from God. The father of worry is our adversary, who wants to devour us. Peter warns us that Satan is like a roaring lion that is starving for evil. He wants to take our minds and eyes off the Father, who is in control of all things. Discouragement, hopelessness, and inadequacy are tools that he uses frequently. Feelings of being not good enough or the need to prove ourselves worthy to others is the way of the world and the devil. God wants us to cast all of our cares on Him. God is the one with the plan.

I am a planner freak, my favorite being the Franklin Covey brand. Every day I write down my prioritized task list, and each week I use my compass and write in all activities and weekly needs. I use a tickler file (an organization file by month and day) in my office, yet I still feel hopelessly unorganized, overwhelmed, and inadequate.

First Peter 5:7 is a familiar verse for most Christians, but do we read it and do it? "Casting all your care upon Him, for He cares for You." I know I still try to do things on my own once in a while, and that's when the feelings of fear, worry, and strife take over.

In Mark 4, verses 35–41, the account of Jesus calming the storm with His disciples is recorded. It had been an exhausting day of teaching for Jesus, and He went right to sleep once they got into the boat. The storm started to build and got to the point that it was raging. The disciples feared for their lives, and Jesus . . . well, Jesus was sleeping!

The disciples woke Jesus up because they were completely terrified. In verse 39, the Bible says, "Jesus stood up and commanded the wind and said to the waves, 'Quiet! Be still!' Then the wind stopped and it became completely calm." The disciples were amazed, confused, and still afraid.

How could Jesus sleep through the storm? I think that Jesus had already learned what it meant to cast all His care on His Father and not worry. He knew God was in control. Jesus was sent to earth to serve as a human example of complete trust in the Father. He never doubted in His Father's love or His ability to care for Him.

In 2 Timothy 2:2–3, 10 Paul wrote to Timothy: "You should teach people whom you can trust the things you and many others have heard me say. Then they will be able to teach others. *Share in the troubles we have like a good soldier of Christ Jesus.* . . . So I patiently *accept* all these *troubles* so that those whom God has chosen can have the salvation that is in Christ Jesus. With that salvation comes glory that never ends" (emphasis added).

How do people know you trust Christ for your every need? They *watch* you during times of adversity and trials. They watch to see if your faith is real or fake. We have to learn to accept trouble and ask God to take care of us. We have to ask God to guide us to make the right decisions and to be true examples of Christian love no matter what.

Jesus said, "Quiet! Be still!" The wind and the waves stopped. We need to cry out to the Father for help, and He will give us whatever we need to persevere. I believe this particular storm was created to allow the disciples to witness God's power at work through His Son, Jesus.

We need to search the Scriptures diligently to find the answers to our questions, our daily concerns, and God's mission for our lives. All the planning in the world won't help if we aren't focused on the mission that God has designed for our lives. I have to remember that when I don't get everything finished on my prioritized list, sometimes God has interruptions intended so that I can witness to those He has chosen. Sometimes those interruptions are to show the love of Jesus through a listening ear, to share the gospel with a lost soul, or to serve as an example of how much I trust God with the challenges of being a leader.

"For we are God's handiwork, created in Christ Jesus to do good works, which God prepared in advance for us to do" (Ephesians 2:10 NIV). If God has prepared things in advance to bless us and to help us succeed as His ambassadors, how do we know the plan? Where do we find the answers? How do we, with godly wisdom, strategize our attack on problems? Hebrews 4:12 states, "For the word of God is living and powerful, and sharper than any two-edged sword, piercing even to the division of soul and spirit, and of joints and marrow, and is a discerner of the thoughts and intents of the heart" (NKJV).

I already indicated that I use a daily planner to organize my life. In my Franklin Covey, right on the back of my compass bookmark, I have a list of questions to help me with decision-making. I wish I could say that I use it faithfully for every decision every day. However, I truly believe that when we seek God's wisdom first, we cannot be stopped. I have listed the questions for each of you as food for thought.

Decision-Making Checklist:
1. Have I prayed about it?
2. Is it consistent with the Word of God?
3. Can I do it and still be a positive Christian witness?
4. Will the Lord be glorified?
5. Am I acting responsibly?
6. Is it reasonable? (Philippians 4:8–9). We are to think and practice what we know to be true.
7. Does a realistic opportunity exist?
8. Are unbiased, spiritually sensitive associates in agreement?
9. Do I have a sanctified desire?
10. Do I have peace about it?

You may be saying, "I try to read the Bible, but it just doesn't make sense to me. It's easier to just have the pastor explain it to me during church." I can't even tell you for sure how many times I have heard this exact excuse for not spending time daily in God's Word. But I can tell you that once I made the decision to make it a priority to find time for Bible study and prayer, my understanding and ability to hear God's voice greatly increased. In fact, if I don't start my day with the Lord, by noon I am craving time alone with Him.

Another excuse often used is, "I'm just too busy with my schedule. I have a job, a husband, and several children. I need to clean the house, take the kids to piano lessons and basketball practice, pick up the groceries…" I think you get my drift. Busyness is another tool of Satan; with our "fast service" world, it is quite effective against both Christians and non-Christians. An acronym that I heard that reminds me of how easily we can forget to make time for the Lord is "Busy Under Satan's Yoke."

In Isaiah 30:21, we are told, "Whether you turn to the right or to the left, your ears will hear a voice behind you, saying, 'This is the way; walk in it'" (NIV). I have found that asking for the Holy Spirit's guidance before I even open my Bible to read makes a huge difference in how clearly I hear the Lord speaking.

Proverbs 9:10 says, "Wisdom begins with respect for the Lord, and understanding begins with knowing the Holy One." At first glance and through a human perspective, it is amazing to me that there are so many people who lack common sense. Then, when I put things into a godly perspective, there are fewer people in the world who seek the wisdom of God than people who think they are wise and have personal agendas for their lives. Arrogance runs rampant in our society and many times is the cause of poor decisions.

"Pride leads only to shame; it is wise to be humble" (Proverbs 11:2). How many times have you tried to talk to someone about a situation or been asked for advice, only to have that person talk *at* you? It drives me crazy when I am asked how to handle a situation but then am interrupted several times with excuses as to why my suggestions will not work. At this juncture of the conversation, I try to just close my mouth and let the person ramble on until they are through complaining.

Let me add one of my friend's thoughts here after she read this chapter. She reminded me that often times people only want to be heard; they really do not want advice. Their pleas are just a way to be heard. I have to remind myself that complaining isn't always complaining; sometimes it's just that you are the only one who will listen to the person.

So why do people ask for advice but seldom listen to it? I think this is because wisdom can be gained only by first putting God's will in our lives, and then God will open our eyes and ears to truth. We will understand how to handle difficult situations only through the guidance of the Holy Spirit.

"At the square by the Water Gate Ezra read the Teachings [Bible] out loud from early morning until noon to the men, women, and everyone who could listen and understand. All the people *listened carefully* to the Book of Teachings. Ezra the teacher stood on a high wooden platform that had been built just for this time.... They read from the Book of the Teachings of God and explained what it meant so the people understood what was being read" (Nehemiah 8:3–4a, 8, emphasis added).

In this Scripture passage, one of the most important things to me is that they *listened*. You cannot understand if you don't listen carefully. In my earlier example, if we ask for advice but never stop talking, we will not hear. This is also applicable in prayer. If we bring our requests to the

Lord but do not take the time to wait quietly, we will not receive answers from the Lord.

The Israelites were searching for answers in the Book of Teachings. They were looking for help upward. In today's society with television, Internet, and other resources, it is so easy to get caught up in what the "experts" of the world say. In fact, in my own quest for perfection and being the best principal that I can possibly be, I have read many self-help books that had excellent ideas and sound advice. However, the ones that truly are applicable are those that are based on Scripture.

If you truly want to be wise, you must look to the Bible. The book of Proverbs is full of wisdom, situations that apply to daily living, warnings, and blessings for godly living, as well as ways to apply understanding of God's Word to our lives. For the past few years, I have made it a practice to read a chapter in Proverbs every day of each month. There are thirty-one chapters and thirty-one days in most months. I read the chapter that coincides with the day of the month and select a new verse each month for meditation on that day. Proverbs has truly become one of my favorite books of the Bible.

"Without leadership a nation falls, but lots of good advice will save it" (Proverbs 11:14). Each of us has been selected to lead in our homes, in our school districts, in our communities, or in our places of work. For me, if I don't teach people (teachers, students, parents, grandparents, community members) to step up and lead, projects will fail, students will drop out, and ideas will never be realized. But with lots of good advice (daily Bible reading and prayer), they will be saved.

Where can you find real answers? In my personal search for God's purpose and mission for my life, I felt it was necessary to set life goals. My life goals were designed to place God as my ultimate authority. I have validated these goals through prayer, as well as used Scripture to authenticate a visionary purpose.

My Four Life Goals:
1. Love the Lord with all my heart: "Trust in the LORD with all your heart, and don't depend on your own understanding. Remember the LORD in all you do, and he will give you success" (Proverbs 3:5–6).
2. Love my husband: "Wives, yield to your husbands, as you do to the Lord" (Ephesians 5:22 NCV).
3. Raise my children to love and be obedient to God's laws: "Always remember these commands I give you today. Teach them to your children, and talk about them when you sit at home and walk along the road, when you lie down and when you get up. Write them down and tie them to your hands as a sign. Tie them on your forehead to remind you, and write them on your doors and gates" (Deuteronomy 6:6–9).
4. Work for the Lord: "In all the work you are doing, work the best you can. Work as if you were doing it for the Lord, not for people" (Colossians 3:23).

Also, I have made it a priority to spend time listening for God's voice. In Psalm 46:10, the Bible states, "Be still, and know that I *am* God; I will be exalted among the nations, I will be exalted in the earth" (NKJV)!

How do we hear the voice of God in order to be obedient? As I stated earlier in this chapter, we must learn to be active listeners. A time for listening is a difficult thing to accomplish if you have an active schedule. However, God has taught me to turn off the radio in the car and listen while I drive to activities and meetings, and to utilize even my car time for Him. If you are a commuter to work, ask God to talk with you during that drive.

In Matthew 25:34–36, Jesus says, "Then the King will say to those on His right hand, 'Come, you blessed of My Father, inherit the kingdom prepared for you from the foundation of the world: for I was hungry and you gave Me food; I was thirsty and you gave Me drink; I was a stranger and you took Me in; I was naked and you clothed Me; I was sick and you visited Me. I was in prison and you came to Me'" (NKJV).

God will speak to you directly when you make time to listen. I have been blessed greatly when God has asked me to do random things during the day. I start my day in prayer and ask God to walk with me at work. I ask Him to speak to me through people, circumstances, or with a still, small voice. I love when something happens at school (good or bad) and I know without a doubt that it's not a coincidence, but a God-thing. When we are actively listening, He gives us ears to hear and eyes to see.

I have learned to be God-confident, not self-confident. I also remind myself often that wherever God is working, Satan is lurking. We have to be ready to encourage others to rely on God, not self. As Hebrews 3:12–14 says, "So brothers and sisters, be careful that none of you has an evil, unbelieving heart that will turn you away from the living God. But encourage each other every day while it is 'today.' Help each other so none of you will become hardened because sin has tricked you. We all share in Christ if we keep till the end the sure faith we had in the beginning."

Discouragement is one of the enemy's biggest and most powerful weapons. I am amazed at how many times something awesome happens. Yet the downside to the situation (or someone telling you that you could have or should have handled a tough situation better) can bring you down before you can even celebrate the positives.

In Nehemiah 6 and 7, the Israelites were diligently working to rebuild the walls of Jerusalem. Over and over Satan sent messages to frighten Nehemiah, to discourage him, and to try to get Nehemiah to give up and to stop doing God's work.

Do you ever feel like you have so many interruptions that maybe something isn't God's will? Rethink this; maybe you are right in the middle of a huge mission for God and Satan doesn't want you to complete it. If the task seems too great or impossible, it could be a God-sized problem, but you are trying to do it alone.

In all cases, take time to read your Bible, meditate on the Word, pray about the job to be completed, act upon God's guidance, and wait for God to finish the work. When you know it's God's plan and you have prepared for the battle, remember your job: "having done all, to stand" (Ephesian 6:13b NKJV). God wants us to stand firmly on His Word, encourage others, and never give up.

Our power is nothing versus God's power. There is absolutely nothing we can humanly do that is good enough. King Solomon came to this realization in Ecclesiastes 2:11: "But then I looked at what I had done, and I thought about all the hard work. Suddenly I realized it was useless, like chasing the wind. There is nothing to gain from anything we do here on earth." As I stated before, we must be God-confident, not self-confident.

Certainly, we will have times that God will test our faith and challenge us to be obedient. Without trials and adversity, we do not truly understand what it means to look to the Father for the answers. God needs obedient servants to accomplish His will. James 4:17 says, "If anyone, then, knows the good they ought to do and doesn't do it, it is sin for them" (NIV). Also, John 16:33 says, "These things I have spoken to you, that in Me you may have peace. In this world you will have tribulation, but be of good cheer, I [Jesus] have overcome the world" (NKJV).

During the heat of the storm, I think we all sometimes think, "Is God angry with me?" At the worst point or when we just can't see a way out of a situation, many of us cry out to the Lord, "Are You there?" However, Psalm 30:5, 11 says, "His anger lasts only a moment but his kindness lasts for a lifetime. Crying may last for the night, but joy comes in the morning. ... You changed my sorrow into dancing. You took away my clothes of sadness, and clothed me in happiness."

The above verses in Psalms promising His kindness for a lifetime give me hope. The promise that my crying will become joy at the end of the journey gives me grace and peace to face any adversity I have been called to deal with today, next week, in a year, or even ten years from now. Even if God is angry at my disobedience in a situation, once I have asked for forgiveness, He promises that His kindness is forever.

As I look back over some of the difficult circumstances God has already brought me through, I am reminded that I have felt God's presence at some of the lowest points in my life. Reflecting on one of those times almost twelve years ago, I can still remember crying in pain all night long because I knew something was wrong with me, but I didn't know what. I went to doctors several different times, but they could not figure out what was causing my pain—and it just kept getting worse. There were several times that I got up to take a hot bath in the middle of the night because that seemed to be the only thing that brought any relief. However, every day God gave me enough strength to get through at work. During that period of time, I truly learned what it meant to rely upon God's strength and provision daily.

After about six months of sleepless nights and constant pain, I was finally diagnosed with rheumatoid arthritis. Thankfully, I was sent to a specialist, and the medications I was given helped control the swelling and the pain in my joints. At the time, I was thankful to finally know what was medically wrong with me. Rheumatoid arthritis, though painful, is not terminal. I found joy not only through my pain (knowing the deep presence of God), but also through finding help medically for my condition.

Since I am a principal, each school year brings many different daily challenges. I just finished my twenty-seventh year in education, and I know that I continually need God's guidance to serve people in a godly manner. When we are called to a leadership role, the adversity we face will be greater; however, we also become a greater threat to Satan.

James 3:1 warns us, "My brethren, let not many of you become teachers, knowing that we shall receive a stricter judgment" (NKJV). It is important that we continually encourage each other. As King Solomon wrote, "As iron sharpens iron, so people can improve each other" (Proverbs 27:17).

In my opinion, educators are held to a higher standard. It is discouraging when students are not treated fairly. There are times that I have had to have difficult conversations with teachers, staff, and parents about adjustments that are needed. The issues that students face today require leaders to build relationships more than ever before. As educators, we need to remember that we are encouragers to our students and future leaders of this world. It is an awesome responsibility. And as parents, we need to equip and train our children to face challenges and adversity by using godly wisdom.

"There is a time to cry and a time to laugh. There is a time to be sad and a time to dance. There is a time to throw away stones and a time to gather them. There is a time to hug and a time not to hug. There is a time to look for something and a time to stop looking for it. There is a time to keep things and a time to throw things away. There is a time to tear apart and a time to sew together. There is a time to be silent and a time to speak" (Ecclesiastes 3:4-7).

"Oh Lord, let our hearts be open to Your perfect timing for all situations." This is my prayer for each of you today. Remember to enjoy every season of your life and to look for the life lessons that God has presented for your growth.

Do you remember the season before you met Christ? I would compare this to the season when the Israelites were dwelling in Egypt as slaves as a result of their sins. When we try to do things on our own, we can't see the light at the end of the tunnel. The Israelites were in slavery for four hundred years before deliverance. However, they were eventually delivered.

If you are wandering in the spiritual desert, just seek Him with your whole heart. Get to know Jesus personally. Spend time praying, listening, and searching the Scriptures. When it seems like God isn't there, it usually means Jesus is carrying you and patiently waiting for you to turn to Him.

If you are trying to conquer the giants in the Promised Land, remember that God did *promise* the land to you. Give Him the battles, and just be willing to be His instrument in all daily challenges. There may be times of crying and sadness during this season, but *oh, get ready* for the time of dancing and joy God has planned for you.

"Bless the LORD, O my soul; and all that is within me, *bless* His holy name! Bless the LORD, O my soul, and forget not all His benefits: who forgives all your iniquities, who heals all your diseases, who redeems your life from destruction, who crowns you with lovingkindness and tender mercies, who satisfies your mouth with good *things*, so *that* your youth is renewed like the eagle's" (Psalm 103:1–5 NKJV).

When we are radically obedient, no matter the trials or sufferings we face, we will be radically blessed. Only through a personal relationship with Jesus Christ can we come to the Father. If you want real answers to all of life's tough questions, seek Jesus as your Savior and best friend.

Chapter Four

A Perfect "10"?

Striving for excellence in performance is a constant goal in my life. At times those who are close to me have called me a workaholic. Working a twelve- to fourteen-hour day at work and then coming home to take care of everything at home is not uncommon for me.

If I look at it honestly, I know this is somewhat true. I have difficulty just relaxing if I know I haven't accomplished everything on my daily task list. I hate letting people down, and the word *no* hasn't always been in my vocabulary. If I am asked to do something for someone else, I try to the best of my ability to fulfill the request. No wonder I am so tired all the time.

I have always wanted to be the best teacher, the best coach, the best administrator, the best friend, the best wife, the best mother, and for the past twenty years, I have really wanted to be the best Christian to those around me. At times I have fallen extremely short of this goal in each of these areas, and it frustrates me.

I remember watching Mary Lou Retton score a perfect ten at the 1984 Olympics. When she was interviewed about this accomplishment and asked how it felt, she said something to the fact it felt just like it had felt every other time. She said she had visualized it in her mind many times before.

A perfect ten score at the Olympics is rare and heralded as the ultimate prize. Similarly, as a young music teacher, I wanted my large group ensembles to receive a "superior" (*I*) rating from all three judges at the district music contest. This was the pinnacle of success in my mind. In 1991, I was in my third year of teaching music and in my first year as a vocal teacher for grades 5–12 in a new school. At district competition that first year, we received three *III*'s, and according to the ratings given to the other fourteen schools competing, we were the worst mixed chorus at the district competition. To make things even harder to accept, I knew we deserved the rating.

In my first year, I had to recruit and recruit to even get kids into choir. When I was hired, I discovered that I had only nineteen students signed up for choir in a class C1-sized school. The previous year in a D2 school district, I had twenty-four students in choir. At my first school, only three students in the whole high school were not in choir, and that was because they were in an agriculture class that period. Nineteen students seemed like slim pickings to me.

Both the instrumental teacher, who had over thirty years of experience teaching music, and I were new to this school system. Unfortunately, several students had lost interest in music as a result of circumstances preceding our arrival. After heavy recruiting tactics and lots of begging (I won't bore you with the details), I had forty students in choir. Of those forty, only eight were boys, and truthfully, only one of them could match pitch... most of the time.

As I was listening to the tapes and comments from the district judges and feeling like a total and complete failure as a musician, my partner in crime gave me these words of encouragement: "Ang, I wouldn't wish your choir on my worst enemy. The judges did not hear your kids at the beginning of the year, so they have no idea how much they have improved. You are doing an excellent job. Put away the tapes and comments from this contest, and move forward."

I really wanted to give up. I had a triple trio (which is a nine girl ensemble), a soloist, and a vocal duet score the coveted *I*. The rest of my small groups and my swing choir received *II*'s, and with the choir getting a *III*, well, my self-esteem was a bit low. I finally resolved that there was nowhere else to go but up.

The next year, my swing choir received a *I* overall with only one judge giving us a *II*, and the choir received a *II* from all three judges. This was definite improvement but, for me, still not good enough.

Just like in athletics, before a program truly becomes your own, you have to diligently teach the skills needed to be successful. During my second year, I started sight-singing as part of our daily rehearsals. By the third year, I had students individually voice test on choral selections as well as take sight-singing tests quarterly.

In my third year, our swing choir began to excel musically. We won trophies at several competitions, and at districts we received straight *I*'s from all judges, as well as the coveted plaque. The mixed chorus was sounding great, too. We did three very difficult pieces, and the kids sang them well. I knew this was the year for a *I* in mixed chorus. The kids were pleased when we finished our performance, and I knew we couldn't have sung any better.

The judges had a split decision. The judge sitting in the middle of the performance hall gave us a "superior" (*I*) rating. He said our choir was well balanced, our literature selections were wonderful, and we showed true performance etiquette in our presentation and actual performance of the pieces we sang.

A Perfect "10"?

The second judge's comments said almost the same thing, except that our altos were overbearing throughout the performance. He gave us an "excellent" (*II*) rating. Guess where he sat in the performance hall? Yes, as you may have guessed, he sat on the side where the altos stood.

The third judge literally tore us apart in his comments. According to him, the tenors were too loud and stretching vocally. The basses weren't strong enough. Instead of doing three pieces, we should have done only two pieces. He also suggested that we select easier pieces to perform. He happened to be sitting closest to the tenors for the performance. He gave us a rating of "good" (*III*).

I had listened to several of the other groups who sang that day. In comparison to what I had heard in earlier performances, I knew we had performed well three musically challenging pieces. I was angry. The third judge taught elementary music in a large school district. It was obvious from his comments that it had been awhile since he had worked with high school voices. Instead of being excited about the positive comments from the other two judges, I could only dwell on the negatives from the third. The overall rating of *II* (excellent) was the only rating that wasn't a superior in all of my performing groups that year, but I still felt like a failure.

Isn't this true in our Christian walk also? Sometimes we strive and strive to do the right things for God, but we forget to ask what things He wants us to do. According to God's Word, all our good deeds seem like filthy rags when compared to the greatness of Christ. However, if God has ordained a specific purpose for our lives, He wants us to work at it with all our hearts to glorify Him.

In Ephesians 6:7–8, the Bible says, "Do your work with enthusiasm. Work as if you were serving the Lord, not as if you were serving only men and women. Remember that the Lord will give a reward to everyone, slave or free, for doing good."

I had done everything I knew to do: from selecting the perfect music for the district contest, to preparing the entrance and exit from the risers, to giving exact instructions for professional dress and, most importantly, rehearsing every section over and over until the kids had learned it correctly and memorized it for a perfect performance. As we were leaving, one student who was a tenor and who was also a perfectionist came up and hugged me. He said, "Mrs. Leifeld, we gave it our best shot. We couldn't have sung any better."

That evening I was venting to my husband about the *III* rating from the one judge. In my frustration I cried, "That's it! From now on, I am going to choose easier music. I am going to do only four-part music like the rest of the choirs. Ken, we did eight-part music well and still got only a *II*."

Ken quietly said, "Why did you choose such difficult music if you can do easier stuff? Do you have to do foreign language and that many parts?"

"If I don't give my students the opportunity to learn challenging literature in high school, they may never get the chance to enjoy singing and hearing quality sound," I retorted. "If I don't teach them to appreciate all styles of music, who will?"

"Are you going to allow one man's opinion to change your whole philosophy of teaching?" Ken asked.

Ken's words hit home. Was I really going to make receiving the "superior" rating my only goal for teaching music? I hate it when he is so blunt ... and truthful ... and *right*. (By the way, if you ask my husband, he will say that he is always right!)

That was the day that a judge's praise ceased being my top priority. In April 1993, I decided to stop working for praise from men and start concentrating on glorifying God by continuing to teach with enthusiasm. I was going to continue to select tough and challenging pieces. Don't get me wrong; performing with excellence was still clearly my goal. But my desire to create a passion for all my students to understand and appreciate all styles of music grew and became my top priority. For the first time, the need to receive a "superior" rating at contest was no longer looming over my head. I also knew that I was not a failure.

In the fall of 1993, I started the first day of school with new passion for enhancing my students' learning experience and expanding their repertoire for quality literature. This was my fourth year in the district, and I knew well the voices of the children returning. I also knew they were ready to be challenged musically.

"O Sifuni Mungu" was the first song of the year to sight-read on the first day of school. If you have taught high school students, doing anything on the first day of school—let alone expecting them to learn a spiritual in Swahili—was a bit of a stretch for them. When the students saw my rehearsal schedule on the board, they started whining and complaining. Students asked me if I had gone crazy over the summer.

"Ms. Leifeld, foreign language on the first day?"

Some students muttered under their breath, while others let me know verbally and with their body language that they were less than thrilled with my challenge. However, they all moved into their places as designated on an assigned seating chart, and we began to sing.

Our first concert that fall included songs in Swahili, Bohemian, Latin, Spanish, and of course English. The concert was well received by our community, and we were off and learning with vigor and excitement. The Swahili piece was by far the students' favorite song from that concert.

As preparations for the district music contest began, I gave the students the two pieces that I had selected for the contest. I also decided to give them the opportunity to collectively select the last piece for competition as an ensemble.

I strategically selected five pieces for the students to sight-read in this selection process: three pieces that I was sure they wouldn't choose, a quality piece that would go well with the other two pieces we were going to perform, and a tough a cappella piece that ended in six parts.

To my surprise, the students almost unanimously selected the toughest piece. I turned around and looked at the students' goals for the year that we had posted on the wall. One of the student goals was to finally receive a "superior" rating in mixed chorus at the district competition. They wanted a trophy.

Because of this goal, I knew that I needed to be straightforward with the kids. I told them that I also really wanted to do the piece "Make a Noise," but they needed to know that I did not believe we could receive a "superior" rating on it. I knew that ending our performance with an a cappella piece that climaxed in six parts, with every part singing in their head voices (which is the upper register of their voice) and the sopranos on a high G, as well as staying in the same key throughout, would be difficult. (I realize that some of this musical stuff might not make sense to all of you, but those of you reading this who have taught music have a better idea of what we were going to have to accomplish.)

I also told them I didn't care what we received as a rating; however, they did, which was apparent by the three goals they had set at the beginning of the school year. I shared with them that I welcomed the challenge of doing the best we could with tough music, if they did. The students agreed.

We worked hard. The other two pieces I had chosen without the students' input for the contest weren't exactly easy, either. The kids pushed themselves, and my section leaders (student leaders) really helped encourage all members of the choir to listen carefully and work together.

The performance was wonderful. I couldn't stop smiling after the final chord of "Make a Noise." They had listened well to each other and gave an outstanding performance. I told my accompanist as we left the performance hall that I was so pleased with the kids, and it just didn't matter what the judges thought.

The ultimate goal had been reached. Students were learning by my example that excellence in performance was in knowing that you did the best you could. They were enthusiastic and ecstatic. They had enjoyed the moment. This learning experience and performance was a perfect ten in my eyes.

We received a "superior" rating and a trophy, but the funny thing is, I never went to look at the judges' sheets. In anticipation, several of the kids hung around at the judges' sheets in the cafeteria. I was told they jumped up and down and hugged one another. I will never forget students running down the hall towards me, yelling, "Mrs. Leifeld, you said we couldn't get a *I* if we did these pieces!"

I smiled and said, "I guess I was wrong."

We left the contest that year with sixteen "superior" ratings and one "excellent" rating from the vocal groups. The mixed chorus and the swing choir got to bring home hardware for the trophy case. The instrumental groups fared just as well in their ratings, and our music department was starting to have a reputation for its performance abilities.

Not only have I struggled with striving for perfection in my professional life, but I have also often struggled with many personal issues. When I take my eyes off Jesus and listen to the world's view, it clouds my vision and priorities. I have often worried about my weight, my lack of beauty, and my abilities as a mother and wife.

The world's view of a perfect ten involves not only being physically perfect, but also stunningly beautiful. The models featured on magazine covers are usually underweight and extremely skinny. I read once that Marilyn Monroe was a size 12. Today's models strive for a size 4 or smaller. Our society's view of beauty has changed so drastically that girls and women struggle with eating disorders more now than ever before.

For years I struggled with my weight and worried about my appearance. I used to step onto the scale every day and scrutinize why I was a pound or two heavier than the day before. I tried crazy diets, exercised excessively, and worried during each pregnancy that I would not get back to my normal figure. I compared myself to those skinny little models on the covers of the magazines, and quite frankly, I didn't measure up too well.

As many of you have probably done, I have stood in front of the mirror, stressing out that this outfit made me look fat or that I didn't have the right body to wear the outfit I wanted to purchase. And of course, if I had to move up a size to purchase a pair of jeans or shorts that I liked, well, just forget it. I didn't need them!

In Matthew 6:25, Jesus states, "So I tell you, don't worry about the food or drink you need to live, or about the clothes you need for your body. Life is more than food, and the body is more than clothes." In verse 28-29, He goes on to say, "And why do you worry about clothes? Look at how the lilies in the field grow. They don't work or make clothes for themselves. But I tell you that even Solomon with his riches was not dressed as beautifully as one of the flowers." Then in verse 33, Jesus tells us what the most important thing to his Father is: the thing you should want most is God's kingdom and doing what God wants. "Seek first God's kingdom and what God wants. Then all these other needs will be met as well."

God already knows my every worry before I look in the mirror. He knows my every fear of failure and rejection. And He tells me that I am beautiful and desirable because I am a woman after His own heart. It has taken me a long time to believe this, but I know without a doubt that the most important thing about me has nothing to do with how I look or the good deeds I have done. I am a daughter of the King, and that is where my reward will be found.

"A wise woman strengthens her family, but a foolish woman destroys hers by what she does" (Proverbs 14:1). I currently serve as a secondary principal. My job is exciting and challenging and at times a bit discouraging. In light of all the commotion I deal with each and every day at school, where is my first priority (after serving the Lord, of course) supposed to be? You guessed it—my family. God calls us to teach and model what it means to be a Christian to our children. I am not talking about saying it; I am talking about living it.

The verse above reminds me of how important modeling and serving Christ fully is for my watching children. Cassie, Jerad, Austin, and Justin need to catch their mother reading her Bible, kneeling in prayer, and sharing the gospel boldly whenever possible. They need to see me standing firm on things that are important, even when my decisions are not popular with the world.

Proverbs 19:18 states, "Correct your children while there is still hope; do not let them destroy themselves." This verse reminds me that I have to stand strong about the kind of music my kids listen to, the kind of movies they watch, the friends they select to hang out with, and the places they choose to go. It frustrates me when parents tell me they let their children make their own decisions. The sad thing is I usually hear this from parents of children who are acting out in any way they can just to get their parents' attention. They are craving discipline because they want to know if they are loved.

One of the reasons I went into education was to reach students who didn't have godly guidance at home. I was so fortunate to grow up in a Christian home and to have parents, who set rules, gave me a curfew, and cared about my spiritual well being. At first I was completely shocked when I learned that the Bible stories that were so ingrained in my upbringing had never been heard by many of the students I encountered. In fact, the number of students who have never been inside a church is growing rapidly in the public school setting.

Now, as an administrator, I daily talk with my teachers and students about the importance of modeling moral behavior in the classroom. Modeling expected behavior, sharing moral values, and living a life of integrity are extremely important, especially in a society that claims to be Christian but doesn't even know what that means. I know that living out God's purpose as a role model for the students I serve at school and for my own children will help them to sense God's call and hopefully seek Christ to learn the purpose for their lives.

My family needs to know through my actions that they are the most important people in my life. Because of my drive for excellence as a professional, I sometimes fail at putting my family ahead of emergencies at school. I pray about kids and situations constantly, especially when I feel inadequate to solve some of the problems that arise. I also know at times I bring those worries home, and it affects how I respond to my kids, sometimes positively but also negatively.

Over the past few years, I have tried diligently to schedule one-on-one time with my children at some time during each week. They don't know it's on my priority list to do each day, but by making this commitment, it helps me focus on asking about their day and finding out what is going on with them personally.

The importance of praying daily for our children is incredible. I have found through doing this that God has protected my children's decisions, given them wisdom and discernment beyond their years on some occasions, and helped them to withstand some pretty high expectations inflicted upon them because they are the principal's kids. Proverbs 14:26 reminds me that serving God wholeheartedly will also benefit my children. It says, "Those who respect the LORD will have security, and their children will be protected." What an awesome promise from God!

The Proverbs 31 woman used to make me feel so inadequate. Not only is she the perfect wife and mother, but also her work is found to be impeccable. Her children call her blessed, her husband trusts her completely, she works with lots of energy, and she speaks wisely. (Her children call her blessed? Yeah, right!)

Who sees us at our worst times? If you are like me, your answer will be "my family." One of my goals at school is never to yell at a student. When I feel my anger rising, I have learned to use strategies to calm myself internally before I open my mouth to speak. Oh, how I wish I could do this better at home, too!

I used to pray for patience. However, whenever I would pray this prayer, I was usually screaming, "And I need it right now!" I have since learned *not* to pray for patience because the only way to receive patience is to endure even more trials and adversity. Believe me, God often uses adversity in my life to get my complete attention.

Anyway, then I read a devotional written specifically about the Proverbs 31 woman. The writer stated that they thought this scripture was meant to encompass many different kinds of women and the strengths they could possess. It went on to explain that no woman could be all of this by herself. My reaction to the devotional was one of thankfulness because I knew I couldn't do all of the things described in those twenty-one verses.

This thought gives me hope to continue to strive to serve God in a way that will honor my husband and my children. It reminds me that outside beauty is not what God looks at. He looks into our hearts and knows whether our desires our godly. It makes me realize that compliments

I receive for my work should be appreciated. God promises that if we live uprightly, He will bless us as well as allow us to receive recognition from others.

Verses 30 and 31 of Proverbs 31 sum it all up for me: "Charm can fool you, and beauty can trick you, but a woman who respects the LORD should be praised. Give her the reward she has earned; she should be praised in public for what she has done." I understand and know that I will never be a perfect ten. However, I truly desire to serve the Lord to the best of my ability through His strength.

Be a wise woman. Strengthen your family with words of encouragement, provide loving arms to hug and comfort them, and model a positive attitude even in negative situations. Only through God's eyes and His grace can we been seen as a perfect "*10*".

Chapter Five

Isn't It Amazing What a Prayer Can Do?

"Pray continually," or "Pray without ceasing" (NKJV), says Paul in 1 Thessalonians 5:17. This is one of the shortest verses in the Bible, yet it holds a strong message. Paul tells us that God wants us to pray constantly. It doesn't say to pray only when we have problems. This verse doesn't say to pray only when we're sad or in despair. It says to pray continually. That means we are to pray and praise God daily and bring our concerns and joys to Him in prayer.

In March of 2002, Ken and I told our children we were going to have another baby. Cassie was ecstatic. Cassie had been begging me for years for another baby brother or sister. She had even offered on several occasions to have a talk with Dad about this baby thing. That evening as I put the kids down for bedtime, Cassie prayed for twins.

I told Cassie that praying for a healthy baby was the best way to pray. This didn't discourage her in the slightest. Every night she prayed for twins. Every night I begged her not to get her hopes up and to be thankful that we were going to have another baby, instead of asking for more.

On the day of my first official appointment for my pregnancy, Cassie gave me a hug and a kiss and said, "The doctor is going to tell you that you are having twins."

I looked at those hopeful and believing eyes and hugged her tight. I said, "I hope you won't be disappointed when I come home and tell you there is only one."

Jerad overheard our conversation and hollered, "Just make it a boy!"

As I waited in the lobby of my doctor's office, I read over a quick devotional. I don't remember the scriptures used or even the gist of the devotional, but the last line was "Prepare yourself for a gift from God that only He can give." I silently prayed, thanking God for giving me this gift. I was very excited about this baby. I had vowed to myself that I was going to enjoy being pregnant this time. I was not going to stress over the weight I gained, how I looked, or let anything steal my joy. God had changed Ken's heart about having another child, and He had allowed me to conceive.

I remember looking at the ultrasound and thinking it looked strange. It looked like two blobs, and I thought, *The placenta can't be that big yet, can it?* I reasoned with myself that it had been over eight years since my last pregnancy, so maybe technology had changed that much.

Then the nurse voiced my concerns out loud. She said, "This looks kind of odd." She continued to move the sensor over my stomach and then said, "Oh my goodness, you are going to have twins!"

I was in complete shock. God had answered the prayers of a little girl. I knew Cassie would be so excited about God answering her prayer. I started to cry. I was so overwhelmed by the news. I didn't know what to say except to ask the nurse if she could tell if they were boys or girls.

When the nurse saw my tears, she apologized for telling me so abruptly. I told her it wouldn't have mattered how she had told me; I was overjoyed, excited, extremely surprised, and I wasn't quite sure how I was going to break the news to my husband. I shared with her that it had taken me eight years to convince Ken that we should have one more baby—and now there were going to be *two*.

She was able to tell from the ultrasound that the babies were boys. She was positive on one of the babies and about 95 percent sure on the second baby.

Jerad had wanted a brother. That's all he had asked for over and over. No girl! When we told the kids we were expecting a baby, Jerad was a bit distraught about the whole thing. His biggest concern was that he didn't want to be "the man in the middle." God had answered Jerad's prayer for a brother.

Why pray? Because God always answers! Cassie's faith was enlarged greatly by God answering her prayer with twin boys. She realized that God does listen to the prayers of children. When she was very young, I heard her tell people about this prayer numerous times. And Ken, well, he asked Cassie why hadn't she prayed to win the lottery instead.

How do we learn about God's unconditional love and mercy? Pray about everything, big or small.

How do we keep from being surprised by trials and adversity? Pray for discernment and guidance in all situations.

How do we keep our desires and needs godly? Pray for a pure heart.

How do we know God's will? Pray for God's wisdom and learn not to lean on our own understanding. Learning to hear God's voice over our own thoughts can happen only through consistent time spent in God's Word daily. It is imperative to make time to sit quietly, pray fervently, and listen intently for His voice.

Over the years, I have met many people who look at prayer as a last-ditch effort. They have already tried everything else and nothing has worked yet, so they think maybe they should pray about it or ask someone to pray for them. Some people think about praying only when they are in a crisis. If things seem to be going well, they forget about God.

I truly feel sorry for people who have not discovered the awesomeness of just being with God in prayer. God is not a lucky charm that we call upon when we have tried everything humanly possible. God wants to be involved in our lives. He wants us to experience His nearness and His unwavering love.

Don't get discouraged if you are just starting to see the importance of prayer in your walk. It has taken me years to learn the importance of "breath prayers." Not only do I try to find a quiet place to be alone and soak up God's goodness, but also I pray during daily chores, at my job, when a new problem arises, and when I need wisdom to make a decision *now*. I also find that when I am driving to the numerous extracurricular activities I am required to supervise, this is an excellent time to reflect and just talk with God.

There are periods of time when life seems full of struggles for me. However, I can say I am not usually surprised by each new trial. Many times God has prepared me to face the tough decisions and wade through the junk to get to the truth. In 1 Peter 4:12, Peter says, "My friends, do not be surprised at the terrible trouble which now comes to test you. Do not think something strange is happening to you." Then in verse 16, he goes on to say, "But if you suffer because you are a Christian, do not be ashamed. Praise God because you wear that name."

When we truly seek to do God's will in our thoughts, our words, and our deeds, Satan is going to try to defeat us. He will use anything he can to stop us from truly realizing God's mission for our lives. He will discourage us, keep us busy and out of the fight, or even use scare tactics.

Second Timothy 3:12 says, "Indeed, all who desire to live a godly life in Christ Jesus will be persecuted" (ESV). If you are enlarging territory for God's kingdom by sharing your faith, praying for others, and serving others to show them Christ, Satan wants to stop you. He will do anything and use anyone and any circumstance he can to keep you from reaching others for Christ.

Second Timothy 2:15 tells us, "Make every effort to give yourself to God as the kind of person he will accept. Be a worker who is not ashamed and who uses the true teaching in the right way." To know God's will, we need to spend time in prayer and in the Word each day. I am not talking about ritualistic worship; I am talking about time with God to get to know Him and His will for our lives. To be used mightily by God (and He can use the weakest of people), we have to make every effort to give our whole hearts to God.

When we spend time in prayer, there are no surprises. We may not know the trial coming, but God will prepare us mentally for the battle. I urge each of you to set aside time alone with your Father each day. "Then he [Jesus] said to his disciples, 'The harvest is plentiful, but the laborers are few; therefore pray earnestly to the Lord of the harvest to send out laborers into his harvest'" (Matthew 9:37–38 ESV). In other words, we need a few good men (and women) who will work with all their hearts, souls, and minds without shame for Jesus Christ.

Psalm 62:8 says "People, *trust* God all the time. Tell him all your problems, because God is our protection" (emphasis added). This passage of Scripture was from my devotions on a particular Wednesday morning as a reminder and reassurance to me. I had met with my accountability partner (someone who holds you spiritually accountable on goals that you have set for yourself in service to God) the Tuesday night before and had encouraged her to trust God completely and to share with Him all of her worries and concerns. I also told her, "God will give us peace and rest when we trust Him completely with everything."

The next morning, God said to me, *Angie, are you trusting me with all of your problems, or are you trying to solve them on your own?*

You see, on Sunday, our boiler at the school went down, so my maintenance guy and I had quality time together. Then on Monday, during the school day, the boiler was down again. Some of our classrooms went below fifty degrees. At one point, the kitchen temperature was at thirty-seven degrees. We had a repairman from our maintenance company at the school who assured me, as he was diligently working to fix the problem, that we would have heat on Tuesday. However, at 6:00 p.m. on Monday night, we were back to square one and unsure as to why the heat wasn't working. We decided to close school on Tuesday. We did not want to have the students endure another day of no heat in the building.

Here is the thing: I had a massive headache on Sunday while we working at the school (I think the headache was caused by a possible gas leak). Another overwhelming headache again Monday because of the added stresses of the boiler situation and no heat for the children, and *not once* did I even think to pray about it. Wow! I had prayed about many other things each morning, but not my real stressors.

Then God gave me verse after verse in my devotions about rest and trusting:

> "I find rest in God; only he can save me. He is my rock and my salvation. He is my defender; I will not be defeated" (Psalm 62:1–2).

> "He who dwells in the shelter of the Most High will *rest* in the shadow of the Almighty" (Psalm 91:1 NIV, emphasis added).

"Let my soul be at rest again, for the Lord has been good to me" (Psalm 116:7 NLT).

In Matthew 6:25–34, Jesus tells us to bring God everything. He tells us that God cares about the lilies of the fields, the birds in the sky, and so of course He cares about the details (problems) in our lives. I guess God thought that I needed a little reminder of that. He wanted me to give Him my worries, my troubles, my concerns, my trials, and my weariness. Through study of these scriptures, once again, He asked me to lay all my concerns at His feet. The promise of rest to a sleep-deprived person was an awesome thought.

I wish I could say the boiler was the only big issue that week, but it wasn't. However, the next morning I read Psalm 64:1: "Hear me, O God, as I voice my complaint; protect my life from the threat of the enemy" (NIV). The threat of the enemy was discouragement, complete weariness, and wondering mentally how I could continue. These were not words from God, but from Satan, that roaring lion that wants to see you and me defeated and discouraged instead of enjoying God's goodness. I poured out my heart in prayer that morning, not only thanking God for His goodness, but also begging for His will to be mine. I asked Him to keep me focused on Him instead of on silly circumstances or situations that were out of my control.

As we were leaving for school, Jerad asked if he could babysit the twins that night instead of going to the game. He said he thought that I might enjoy watching the game, and he sure didn't mind staying home. What a blessing! I was exhausted, and once again God was providing strength. I wouldn't have to chase two toddlers at the basketball game.

Are there things that can get in the way of our prayer lives? The answer is a resounding yes. Sin in our lives is a huge obstacle to prayer. When we love sin more than we love God, it is difficult to pray with a pure heart or to ask for the things of God. Also, our attitudes, our actions, and our lack of faith can keep us from praying. Sometimes pride or thinking that a certain situation is something we should be able to handle on our own is a huge barrier.

Is negativity stealing your power? This statement came to me one morning while I was praying and complaining in the shower. My immediate response was, "Yes, Lord, I have been allowing negativity to bring me down." My question to you is, why is it so much easier to see the things that aren't going the way we want instead of seeing how God is working for our good? I am amazed at how many Christians I meet who seem to only be able to complain about their jobs, their spouses, and their children. I am not saying that there aren't times I want to whine loudly, but I have learned to look for the positive in many ugly situations. Negativity is a killer of joy and peace. It blinds you from God's goodness and His plan for your life, if you are always questioning why.

Another tool of the devil that he uses quite well against us is busyness. At times I have met myself coming and going so much that my alone time with God started lacking. When I don't get enough time in prayer, negativity takes over. I begin to have feelings of despair and want to just give up the fight. I find that when I don't start my day with the Lord, I run out of energy, patience, and love for others.

One day while I was praying on the run and driving to work, a song by Casting Crowns called "Praise You in This Storm" came on K-Love radio. (If you don't listen to K-Love, I highly recommend it! It's 88.1 in my area.) Anyway, God reminded me that He had a purpose for the craziness in my life right then. I needed to praise Him no matter what others were saying or how I was feeling about a given situation.

In Numbers 11:1–10, the Israelites were grumbling about having manna and no meat. The Lord had been providing food daily from heaven, but all they could think about was that the food was not what they had in Egypt. The Bible says they whined, " But now our whole being is dried up; there is nothing at all except this manna *before* our eyes" (verse 6 NKJV).

Can you believe their ingratitude? They had just been delivered from four hundred years of slavery, seen miracles of God's provision in the desert several times, and yet they were complaining. They wanted to go back to Egypt. Unbelievable! They had been praying for deliverance forever, and now they wanted to go back because of food choices? Keep this in mind: in Numbers 11:1a, the Bible says, "When the people complained, it displeased God" (NKJV).

Are we any different? When the going gets tough in our Christian walk, do we follow God's lead unquestioningly, or do we whine about the difficulties we are facing? The Israelites had been freed from hard slavery of more than four hundred years under the Egyptians. In Leviticus 26:13, God promised, "I am the LORD your God, who brought you out of the land of Egypt, that you should not be their slaves; I have broken the bands of your yoke and made you walk upright" (NKJV).

Yet, instead of focusing on their freedom and God's provision in their wilderness wanderings, they began to complain. They complained so much that Moses asked God to just let him die. Even Moses, surrounded by the negativity of the Israelites, forgot about the power he had available to him through his almighty God. I don't know about each of you, but there have been times when I could really relate to Moses' request. It is difficult to be in a leadership role and please people.

Jesus Christ has broken the bondage of slavery to sin through His death on the cross. We are free and able to serve a risen Savior. To be leaders in times of trials and difficulties, we must be followers of Jesus

Christ. There is always a reason for everything that happens to us daily. If we spend all of our time trying to figure out why God is allowing something terrible or difficult to happen to us, we will miss out on all the blessings because we won't be able to see them.

Focus on Christ. Focus on the power over death we have received through Jesus Christ. Live a life of victory instead of defeat. Ask the Holy Spirit to teach you during the storm and to help you keep praising God in everything.

I have come to realize that I learn more about God's provision and His unconditional love during the storms of life than during the calm times. A storm seems to arrive in my life just about the time I think I've got everything under control. Yes, the storms are to remind me that to lead others to Jesus, I must first learn to be a follower. It also reminds me that I can lose my focus to follow God's plan when I take my eyes off Jesus and start listening to the negativity.

Use the power you have been given. The power of prayer is unfathomable. Forget the negatives around you and focus on the positives. Jesus Christ is your spark plug to live a life of victory.

"Pray without ceasing," as Scripture says. If you live a life of prayer, you will never be disappointed. You may be surprised at how God answers. His blessings will far exceed your expectations. You will be amazed at what a prayer will do.

Chapter Six

Finding the Calm in the Storm

I think that for years I was oblivious to how Satan worked to try to trip me up in my walk with Christ. There were many times when things happened around me that I considered unfair or terribly tragic. Because I was a Christian, I wanted (and thought) I deserved the storybook ending of "and they lived happily ever after."

As a babe in Christ, I would cry to the Lord, asking, "Why would You allow this to happen? Lord, where are You? Are You watching what's going on down here? Do You hear me, Lord?"

In Jeremiah 23:23–24, the prophet Jeremiah shares these words with us about God and His sovereignty: "'I am a God who is near,' says the Lord. 'I am also a God who is far away. No one can hide where I cannot see him,' says the Lord. 'I fill all of heaven and earth,' says the Lord." God is always near, and He is always watching. We cannot hide from Him, and He will work all things here on earth and in heaven to bring Him glory. In this passage, God was telling Jeremiah and the Israelites that He was in control.

As a young Christian, I would become especially upset when I knew a person who was suffering sorrow from what seemed to me to be the untimely death of a loved one or a horrific tragedy. It was hard for me to understand how God could allow such pain. I also questioned God when situations of persecution came to a person who was sharing their faith at their workplace. In fact, unfortunately, I have heard about educators who lost their jobs for sharing their faith too boldly. At the time, because I was only looking through my eyes, I had difficulty in understanding why the adversity came. I thought that God should take care of everything concerning Christians' problems.

However, in Romans 8:28, we are told, "We know that in everything God works for the good of those who love him. They are the people he called, because that was his plan." In other words, not everything that happens to us will be good, but all situations will work for our good if we truly love the Lord. I believe this means we are going to have times of joy and peacefulness and times where storms will rage in our lives.

Some storms will be like gentle April showers, where we will still see the goodness of the Lord, but other storms will resemble Hurricane Katrina, where only destruction seems apparent. The thing to remember is that a lesson is always available to be learned in times of adversity and trial. We must be obedient to the Lord by keeping our eyes wide open, our ears carefully listening, and our hands and hearts ready for service.

You see, I never thought about the fact that Satan could be behind a storm and that his entire purpose was to defeat Christians—all of us—spiritually. Think about it. When we are discouraged, disappointed, and at the end of our ropes with our emotions, do we see that God's hand is still working for our good? Satan knows that we are not nearly as effective as witnesses for Christ when we are currently in the battle of our lives that is testing our faith.

First Peter 5:8 says, "Control yourselves and be careful! The devil, your enemy, goes around like a roaring lion looking for someone to eat." In the

NIV version, it states that Satan wants to "devour us," and believe me, he will use every trick in the book to trip us up.

Satan can trip us up in many ways. We need to constantly look into God's Word for encouragement and answers. In Proverbs 3:7–8, the Bible says, "Don't depend on your own wisdom. Respect the LORD and refuse to do wrong. *Then* your body will be healthy, and your bones will be strong" (emphasis added). Also, in Psalm 16:9, we read these words of David: "So I rejoice and am glad. Even my body has hope."

In November 2004, I was diagnosed with rheumatoid arthritis. This was after six months of unexplained pain and being unable to even get out of bed each morning. To make this situation even crazier, up until the flare-up of pain, I was running four miles each morning. I was really enjoying our move to Beaver Lake and the scenery during my morning run.

Then suddenly I couldn't get out of bed. The pain first started in my knees, so I purchased new running shoes. Then my feet would throb not just in the morning, but all day. I began to hobble out of bed to a whirlpool so I could endure the pain. Finally, the pain was in all my joints, including my ankles, hips, elbows, shoulders, neck, jaws, wrists, and fingers.

Where was the calm in this storm? I found I could be thankful for three things:

1. I finally knew what I was dealing with, even if it was an incurable disease.
2. I am special! Only 1 percent of people in the nation have this type of arthritis.
3. I was selected as a person to be involved in a research study. I was in the very early stages of the disease, and they wanted to find out what works best for RA patients. All medications ($1,500 a

month, X-rays, blood tests, eye exams, and visits to the doctor) would be paid for during the entire study.

Oh, how the Lord provides—sometimes even before we know how to ask.

For years, I prayed for whatever it would take for my husband to become the spiritual leader of our household, whatever it would take for my children to know their purpose and God's will for their lives, whatever it would take for me to let my light shine before men and women in a way that brings Him honor. "Lord, use me as You want" was my prayer." Well, an incurable disease never seemed like an answer to my prayers. However, God prepared me for the news and has been my strength.

The two passages I shared earlier, Proverbs 3:7–8 and Psalm 16:9, were given to me as encouragement from the Lord the day after I met with the specialist. The doctor shared that the goal of this study was a very aggressive treatment that would have me in remission within a year. God's promise was to be my hope, my health, and my strength.

Oh, how I am thankful for a loving and caring Father. Be encouraged—God never wastes a hurt or trial. James says we are to "consider it pure joy" whenever we face trials. We have to learn to look for the calm in each storm. We are going to be constantly bombarded with situations, small and great, that can bring us down.

About a month later, God again showed me calm in the storm. In December 2004, right before Christmas break, Cassie began to complain about a sore throat. Trying to take time off from work is never an easy feat, but the last week before break with students is especially difficult. Anyway, I took Cassie to the doctor and found out she had strep throat.

Cassie had a basketball tourney that coming weekend, so I asked the doctor to give her a shot. My thoughts were, *This is Wednesday afternoon, and on Friday night the tourney starts in Grand Island. The shot will help her heal more quickly.* To say the least, Cassie wasn't happy with my suggestion but agreed to two shots instead of pills. The doctor said since she was already starting to feel better, the shots would probably guarantee her feeling well enough to participate in the tourney.

The nurse then asked about my boys. The clinic had been having tons of kids with strep, and with how contagious it can be, they were concerned, especially since the twins were so young. The twins had coughs (as usual), but I didn't think it was anything serious, and Jerad hadn't complained about anything. The nurse clearly stated that if she were in my shoes, she would test all the kids today.

I called the school to get Jerad out of class, and I called the day care to pick up the twins. I brought the boys right back to the office, and you guessed it: all three boys tested positive for strep. Jerad wasn't too pleased with Mom insisting on him having shots when he didn't even have a sore throat and felt absolutely fine. And of course, the twins *loved* being poked!

The doctor also insisted on testing me for strep. With all the medications I was on for rheumatoid arthritis, I couldn't afford to get sick. Praise the Lord, I did not test positive. Believe it or not, they gave me preventive antibiotics. Because my immune system was being shut down in order to get the arthritis under control, they gave me antibiotics and suggested I skip my shots for that week.

"The king [I] truly trusts the Lord. Because God Most High always loves him [me], he [I] will not be overwhelmed" (Psalm 21:7). Then verse 13 in the same psalm says, "Be supreme, Lord, in your power. We sing and praise your greatness."

How did I find the calm in this small storm?

1. Well, Cassie was already on the mend, though still contagious. She volunteered to watch the twins so I could go to work and finish the last day of school before break.
2. I had been so rundown with my rheumatoid arthritis and truly barely making it, but God protected me from strep.
3. I had time at home that Wednesday night to get several things done, since no one could go anywhere.
4. God gave me strength to endure, and through His power I wasn't overwhelmed. At least all of the children had strep at the same time, and we wouldn't have sick children that coming week when traveling for Christmas.
5. I could sing and praise God for His provision in times of sickness. Even though all of my children were sick, God kept me strong to care for them.

The coolest thing about spending time with the Lord each day came with my devotions that followed the next morning. I read in Revelation 21:4, "He will wipe every tear from their eyes. There will be no more death or mourning or crying or pain, for the old order of things has passed away" (NIV). Life on earth is only temporary. We are just passing through, and when we get to heaven, there will be no more pain and no more taking care of sick people, because we will all be healthy. What an awesome promise from the Father during a time with a house full of sick children.

One of the things I have learned to appreciate about God is that His timing is always perfect. "But do not forget this one thing, dear friends: To the Lord one day is as a thousand years, and a thousand years is as one day. The Lord is not slow in doing what he promised—the way some people understand slowness. But God is being patient with you. He does not want anyone to be lost, but he wants all people to change their hearts and lives" (2 Peter 3:8–9).

In the spring of 2002, my devotions for almost two weeks straight were based upon preparing for a storm. At the time, things seemed to be going great. My marriage to my husband, Ken, was wonderful. We had also just found out I was expecting a baby. (we hadn't told anyone yet about the pregnancy and we also didn't know that we were going to have twins at this time.) Things at school seemed to be running smoothly. As I read each day's devotional, I prayed and thanked God for all the good things in my life.

I had wanted to have another child desperately. It took eight years to convince Ken that we should, but God granted my request and changed Ken's heart. I knew that with the difficulties I experienced with my two previous pregnancies, I had to be careful and follow all the doctor's instructions. I thought the storm that God was preparing me for was a pregnancy along with my busy schedule. I therefore prayed for God to help me slow down and take care of myself so as not to jeopardize this baby.

Suddenly I realized I needed to ask for wisdom, discernment, and real strength because I sensed God was preparing me for a trial, and it was a big one. On a Sunday night, my nightmare began. A close friend of mine from my church called to warn me about the school board meeting on Monday night. She shared that a large group of people were coming to complain about me to the board members. I hung up the phone and fell to my knees with my Bible and cried to the Lord. I couldn't stop crying because I was so scared. The FEAR inside me was welling up: F (false) E (evidence) A (appearing) R (real). Satan's attack on my mind was great.

Then my Bible miraculously fell open to Psalm 40, which reads, "I waited patiently for the Lord. He turned to me and heard my cry. He lifted me out of the pit of destruction, out of the sticky mud. He stood me on a rock and made my feet steady. He put a new song in my mouth, a song of praise to our God. *Many people* will see this and worship him. Then they will trust the Lord" (verses 1–3, emphasis added).

I didn't know what the accusations were going to be. I didn't know what I had done to offend, but the verses were correct. I didn't even know who was coming to make the accusations. There were "many people" at the board meeting. In fact, the room was full, and I didn't know who was there to speak against me or who just happened to be attending the meeting. I silently prayed for strength as false accusations were said about me. Slanderous statements that had no factual backing were later printed in the local newspaper as facts, broadcasted on TV, and discussed at professional meetings I had to attend. I begged God not to let these people see me cry or for me to show any sign of weakness.

During that meeting, only God protected my heart, because no one stopped those people from speaking. My husband stood in the back of the room, feeling helpless but trying to give me moral support. Our board agenda had a section for "unscheduled audience," and this was the forum they used to air rumors. To be honest, it was one of the most difficult times in my life. I can only praise God for holding me up and keeping me resting in His arms of grace.

To put this into perspective, at the previous board meeting, I had received compliments from all six board members for the way I handled adverse situations, my integrity, and attention to detail. They had voted 6-0 to rehire me for the coming school year. Each member had specific compliments about my leadership and willingness to handle tough situations. I knew without a doubt that what I was experiencing now was a spiritual attack.

In the executive session with the board, they commended me for staying calm in the storm. We discussed the accusations at length, and at the end of the session I announced I was pregnant. It was a long night. I finally cried when I got home. Thankfully, God had prepared me for the attack through Scripture, through prayer, and through a faithful servant of His who called to give the warning.

The next day, I opened an e-mail from one of my best friends and a sister in Christ. She had had a dream that plagued her all night long. She knew that something was going to happen to me. God had revealed to her that I needed prayer because I was going to be attacked with some type of accusations. She didn't know what the accusations were or when it was going to happen, but it was coming soon. Her e-mail described the exact situation from the night before.

Anyway, God shared with her the verses in Luke 22:31–32: "Simon, Simon, Satan has asked to sift you as wheat. But I have prayed for you, Simon, that your faith may not fail. And when you have turned back, strengthen your brothers" (NIV). Her e-mail said, "Angie, Satan has asked to test you, and lots of people will be watching to see if your faith is real. They are going to watch to see if you truly believe what you say about God. They want to see how well you stand up when the rubber hits the road." She went on to say she was praying for me, and she knew that God would carry me through. She also encouraged me to continue to love my enemies. (I still have this e-mail, and on days when I feel overwhelmed by daily events, I look back at it and thank God for His goodness to me.)

Another sister in Christ, who was from my church, gave me encouragement when I needed it most. She said, "As I read about these ridiculous accusations toward you and wondered why this was happening, God said to me, 'Why isn't this happening to more Christians? Satan attacks Christians who are making an impact on society.'" Until that moment, I had been questioning what I had done wrong to deserve such adversity. To this day, I praise God for bringing me through this storm and for sending messengers to keep me focused on Christ instead of on the battle.

Unfortunately, this board meeting was just the first of a long line of attacks from my adversaries. One of the things I had to endure was a six-hour trial with the Nebraska Department of Education to fight for my teaching/administrative certificate. Because of this attempt against my certificate, I was advised by my lawyer not to comment on anything. The media coverage was a bit disheartening, with the television cameras even appearing at my home to film where the principal in question lived. It was difficult for my children as well as for my husband.

At times I felt helpless. I knew that I couldn't worry about this situation; I had to take care of this baby and myself. This was my third pregnancy, and I had been unable to carry my first two children to full term. With my oldest, Cassie, I had spent two full weeks in the hospital on complete bed rest. My pregnancy with Jerad had not been much easier. But God had given us two healthy children, and I had always felt extremely blessed for His provision in this area.

I did the only thing I could do. I gave it to God. First Peter 5:7 says, "Casting all your care upon Him for He cares for you" (NKJV). God gives us unexplainable joy and peace when we give Him all of our cares and worries. I believe it because it happened to me. In the midst of this huge and raging storm, God blessed me beyond my imagination. It was in April 2002 when we found out we were going to have twins. He gave us a gift that I would have never even dreamed of asking for (although as I stated earlier, Cassie prayed for twins every day).

Remember, I started this story by talking about God's timing being perfect. I didn't think so at the time, but because of the news of the twins, I knew that my job was to take care of me. I knew that I had to turn everything over to God. I had to believe that He was in control.

Finding the Calm in the Storm

In Lamentations 3:22–23, the Bible says, "The LORD's love never ends; his mercies never stop. They are new every morning; LORD, your loyalty is great." Daily God proved to me that His love for my family was incredible. He was faithful in His protection of me not only physically, but also emotionally and mentally. God had asked me to obediently serve Him as a principal by upholding the student handbook and living a life worthy of His calling. God had taught me to go to Him each morning for guidance and support. God gave me peace during the fight for my certificate and the attack by those who had been blinded by Satan, and He even gave me the ability to "be still" in the hospital until the boys were born.

On the morning of August 30, 2002, my lawyer called to tell me that all charges had been dropped by the Nebraska Department of Education because of lack of evidence. My certificate as an educator was still intact. Miraculously, people who were supposed to witness against me had a change of heart. Accusations that were made proved to be false, and I was found to be doing my job as a principal in upholding the rules of the student handbook.

In the afternoon on August 30, 2002, after I had spent thirty-six days in the hospital on complete bed rest, Austin Benjamin and Justin Gabriel were born. In the calm of the storm, there is life abundant in Christ. This was by far the most difficult pregnancy for me, but God carried me through in more ways than I can even begin to share.

When the waves of the storm are so great that you can't see above them, dive down under the waves and into the calm. If we have Christ living within us, He will be our calm in every storm. With one command, Jesus can calm any storm. As Matthew 8:26 says, "Jesus answered, 'Why are you afraid? You don't have enough faith.' Then Jesus got up and gave a command to the wind and the waves, and it became completely calm."

God has brought me through numerous storms, some which are at times still painful to remember. I have come to realize that some of those moments of great conflict or severe adversity were due to my lack of obedience, and God needed to get my attention. It's painful to face trials, especially when you know they are meant as discipline. However, many of the storms I have endured have been to strengthen my faith and my personal walk with Jesus. In fact, these storms have strengthened my walk to the point that as I have already stated before I can't even imagine starting my day without time alone in His Word.

There are going to be storms. Look for the calm in the storm. Look to Jesus. He will always carry you when the waves are too rough and the sea is raging. Every storm has a purpose. That purpose is to learn to trust and love the Lord more. It is to learn to walk with confidence in the Lord when everything else around you seems chaotic and out of control. Remember, God is in control. Fix your eyes upon His Son and know peace.

Chapter Seven

What Kind of Love Is This?

Genesis 1:27–28 says, "So God created man in His *own* image; in the image of God He created him; male and female He created them. Then God blessed them, and God said to them, 'Be fruitful and multiply; fill the earth and subdue it; have dominion over the fish of the sea, over the birds of the air, and over every living thing that moves on the earth'" (NKJV).

Sometimes I wonder if God ever asks Himself why He wanted to have children. Think about it. He knew before He even created Adam and Eve that we would sin, and be disobedient, and act defiantly, and throw fits, and yet . . . He loved us enough to have a plan in place for our salvation before we were even born. What kind of love is this? How can God love us as unconditionally as He does?

God desired to create man to be like Him, in His own image. He wanted to look at us and see Himself living in us. God created man and woman to be a reflection of His holiness, His grace, and His love. He created us because He loved that much.

"Therefore a man shall leave his father and mother and be joined to his wife, and they shall become one flesh" (Genesis 2:24 NKJV). God wanted to teach us about unconditional love by creating marriage. On numerous occasions in the New Testament, marriage is used as a metaphor for the love of Christ for His church. Marriage is to be the perfect relationship between a man and a woman with God at the center.

"Then I, John, saw the holy city, New Jerusalem, coming down out of heaven from God, prepared as a bride adorned for her husband" (Revelations 21:2 NKJV). John compares Jesus' return to a beautiful bride before her bridegroom on their wedding day. Do you remember the day you stood at the back of the church, looking at your husband-to-be for his approval? I remember it as if it were only yesterday. Until the day I die, I will remember Ken's smile and the way he looked in his tuxedo. The adoring look a bride receives from her husband-to-be on that day does not even begin to compare to the way God looks at each of us.

We also are given the desire to have children; our own children to raise that will have their father's eyes or mother's nose. God blessed Adam and Eve and told them to multiply and be fruitful. We are a compliment to God's supreme workmanship and omnipotent power.

"Train up a child in the way he should go, and when he is old he will not depart from it" (Proverbs 22:6 NKJV). For parents, it can be difficult to show unconditional love to their children. I truly believe the toughest job ever invented is parenthood. There are no manuals that come with a baby when it is born. No baby is the same in any way. Even twins are totally different and have individual personalities. At times parenting is a ton of trials with several opportunities to make errors, as well as a constant reminder to pray for patience, understanding, and the ability not to strangle that child who just did the exact opposite of what we asked.

Have you ever heard a mom say to her daughter, "Mommy loves you for being so good"? Or a dad tells his son after the big game, "I am so proud of how you played today. We love you very much!"

What Kind of Love Is This?

As a toddler, my son Justin said to me on too many occasions, "Do you love how good I am being? Do you love me, Mommy, for being such a big boy?" Or better yet, "I'm being better than Austin, Mommy. Don't you love it when I am so good?"

These statements usually happen when Austin was crying because he had spilled his milk, broken something, or was just being plain naughty. Plus, oh my goodness, each child is unique and responds completely differently to discipline tactics. As young boys, Austin would melt and beg for forgiveness if I gave him the motherly look or even raised my voice to him. And Justin . . . well, let's just say it took more than "the look."

"Even a child is known by his deeds, whether what he does is pure and right" (Proverbs 20:11 NKJV). As children, most of us learn at a very young age that if we want to be in good graces with our parents, we must first "be good" or do something that makes our parents proud. As a child, I wanted to please my parents. I wanted to be the best at everything so they would be proud that I was their daughter. This desire to please did keep me from getting into too much trouble throughout my growing-up years and has also kept me focused and goal-oriented as an adult.

Honoring our parents is a commandment from God with a promise. In Exodus 20:12, the Bible states, "Honor your father and your mother, that your days may be long upon the land which the LORD your God is giving you" (NKJV). Growing up in a Christian home, I knew the importance of obeying my parents, not only because my dad said so, but also because God says so. I grew up being more fearful of God's wrath than cognizant of His unconditional love. It wasn't until I was older and able to really study God's Word that I realized how many blessings God gives to obedient children.

Don't get me wrong. I don't think we as parents intentionally try to put guilt trips on our children to perform better, but we do. We place pressure on our children to perform, to behave appropriately and, for goodness' sake, do not to embarrass us in front of a bunch of people. As I get older and hopefully better at this parenting role, I apologize more, try to criticize less, and daily give godly encouragement for making the right choices. I have also realized that saying less is more.

To be completely honest, all four of our children as youngsters talked incessantly, sang constantly, and let their presence be known at all times by loudly wrestling or fighting with one another. What did I expect? I certainly wasn't quiet as a child. When the kids were small, believe me—if it was quiet, I knew I'd better start searching for kids because they were up to something, and probably not something good.

When Cassie was only three (and younger!), Ken and I would cringe during the children's sermon each Sunday. Cassie loved being the center of attention. She enjoyed telling stories, and she was good at it. If she raised her hand to speak or answer the pastor's question, we would begin to sink down in the pew and pray. On numerous occasions, our church family got the opportunity to hear about our arguments, her getting a spanking, or whatever else happened to be in her memory bank for the day. After church, all the older ladies would say, "Angie, don't worry! We have all been there. Aren't children a riot?"

Does God ever shake His head or worry about what we are going to say? No, He knows we are going to say the wrong thing before we even say it. Again, what kind of love is this? How can God be so extravagant in His love for a sinner? God is our ultimate example of how to be the perfect parent. He listens to us when we whine, He comforts us when we cry, and He disciplines us when we go astray.

Jerad once asked me why I ever wanted to have children. He emphasized in this conversation that he had no desire to have children at this point or anytime in the near future. Ironically, at his age (I think he was about twelve at the time), I babysat for a family who had four children, and I remember I didn't have any desire to have children of my own, either. I just smiled at Jerad and said, "I can't remember why!"

I have to admit that even on the worst days, I can't imagine life without any of them. They make me laugh when I have had a tough day at work, and when they hug and kiss me, I can't think of anything better than being a mother. Truthfully, I can't even remember what our lives were like before children. I hurt when they hurt. I cry when they cry. And most importantly, when they were young I slept when they slept!

Austin and Justin's newest phrase at age two was "Daddy, I'm stealing your love!" They exclaimed this whenever they were hugging or kissing me. And if I kissed Ken . . . "Daddy! Stop stealing my love!" The best part was both Ken and I received numerous kisses and hugs from them, so the love was "all even" between us. As I reminisce about those early years, I am grateful that at age thirteen, these boys still give hugs and kisses to us often.

I am constantly amazed at the ways God reveals His love for us on a daily basis. His love is unbelievable, unimaginable, unchanging, and unstoppable. There isn't anything we can do to deserve it less, or even more, for that matter. While we were yet sinners, He sent His Son to die on the cross for our sins—yes, His only Son to die a cruel and undeserving death for us. This gift alone is enough to show His unconditional love.

Jesus was God's most extravagant gift to the world. Jesus was God as a man modeling how to love people unconditionally. Jesus loved people so intensely that those who followed Him displayed extravagant love in return.

One of my many favorite stories in the Bible is about Mary Magdalene and her offering of extravagant worship for her Master. She didn't care what people thought of her. Jesus had shown her unimaginable forgiveness, and she wanted somehow to demonstrate to Jesus how much she loved Him in return.

"And behold, a woman in the city who was a sinner, when she knew that Jesus sat at the table in the Pharisee's house, brought an alabaster flask of fragrant oil, and stood at His feet behind *Him* weeping; and she began to wash His feet with her tears, and wiped *them* with the hair of her head; and she kissed His feet and anointed *them* with the fragrant oil" (Luke 7:37–38 NKJV).

In front of a house full of people, she kissed and washed Jesus' feet with her own hair, her tears, and expensive perfume. Because of her reputation, the men were appalled and critical of the way she wasted the perfume. None of these people thought much of the woman, except that she was foolish, but Jesus saw her heart. Jesus took complete control of the situation. He questioned the wisdom of Simon and the others through a parable about creditors and debtors. Then Jesus honored Mary Magdalene for her undying devotion and desire to just be near Him.

> "Then He turned to the woman and said to Simon, 'Do you see this woman? I entered your house; you gave Me no water for My feet, but she has washed My feet with her tears, and wiped them with the hair of her head. You gave Me no kiss, but this woman has not ceased to kiss My feet since the time I came in. You did not anoint My head with oil, but this woman has anointed My feet with fragrant oil. Therefore I say to you, her sins, which are many, are forgiven, for she loved much. But to whom little is forgiven, the same loves little.'

What Kind of Love Is This?

Then He said to her, 'Your sins are forgiven.'" Luke 7:44–48 NKJV

What kind of love is this? It's extravagant! God wants to show His love to us daily. He wants us to be radically obedient so that He can radically bless us. He wants us to desire to be examples of His unconditional love to others around us. He wants us to be His feet, His hands, and His children.

The year 2007 was filled with many difficult situations both professionally and personally, sorrows beyond my comprehension, and God's awesome promise of provision and extravagant love from Him to my family. God brought me through the desert of loneliness, gave me courage in extreme adversity, and strengthened my faith. He fought battles for me in ways that were unbelievable, and because of that, I learned not to question why, but to look for God's hand at work.

We lost my six-month-old niece, Maddison, in March to Leigh's disease. She was the youngest grandchild, and it was very difficult for our entire family. It is amazing how someone so small and so young can have such a large impact on the world. On this day, God gave me incredible strength so that I could sing for her funeral and comfort my brother and his wife. Only through God's strength was I able to give extravagant love to my brother through my voice.

In August, Jerad ran over Justin with our riding lawn mower. From the muffler and blades, Justin received second- and third-degree burns on the entire right side of his face, the back of his head and ears, as well as a spot on his leg. Praise the Lord; Jerad had shut off the blades just moments earlier to tell Justin to get away from the mower while he was mowing. Justin, while running away, tripped over a small tree and fell down behind the lawn mower. Jerad didn't see him and thought Justin had run to the backyard like he told him to do. Jerad backed the mower over the top of Justin.

When I arrived home from work, driving and praying like crazy, Justin was screaming uncontrollably. I called Ken as soon as I realized he was burned. Luckily, he was only moments from the house. We then called an ambulance because we knew we needed to get him to the hospital as quickly as possible. We were not allowed to ride in the ambulance with Justin because of restrictions by the volunteer rescue department. Ken and I tried to follow behind the ambulance in our van; however, the traffic was awful because of rush hour. As we were driving, I called ahead to the hospital to give permission to start treatment as soon as the ambulance arrived. I also called my mom and several prayer warriors and asked them to pray for Justin. I asked them to pray that God would carry him through this ordeal and give him peace.

When we arrived at the hospital, Justin was completely calm and holding a stuffed animal. He looked up and said, "Hi, Mommy. Look what they gave me." Other than his swollen face and large blisters, you would have thought he was perfectly fine.

As my cell phone began to ring off the hook, I heard Ken say to Justin, "Do you want to pray with Daddy for Jesus to help you?" They began to pray together. How awesome it is that we can come to our heavenly Father at any time! Psalm 20 reminds us that we can always call on the Lord: "May the LORD answer you in the day of trouble.... Now I know that the LORD saves His anointed; He will answer him from His holy heaven with the saving strength of His right hand" (Psalm 20:1a, 6 NKJV).

Justin cried only when they gave him a shot for pain. The whole time they scrubbed his face and clipped off the burned skin, he talked to us calmly and was fearless. God held my son tightly. What kind of love is this? It's extravagant.

Ken worked from home for two weeks. I am so thankful that Ken's job was one that he could work from home through the Internet and that his boss was willing to let him. Again God's provision and love for us were shown through details that only God knew we would need.

Because of the severity of his burns, Justin could not attend his first few days of school. For more than a month, Ken and I held Justin down four times a day and scrubbed his face until he bled in order to prevent scarring. It hurt to have to put him through such necessary pain. We then got to move to only twice a day for another two weeks. However, God gave Justin wisdom beyond his five years of age, and he was a trooper. For two years, he wore a safari hat whenever he was outdoors and kept his face moist as suggested by his doctor.

This awful accident allowed Ken and Justin to bond as father and son in incredible ways. Justin often talked about the "special time" he got to spend with just Daddy and him while everyone else was at school. You should have heard them sing the SpongeBob SquarePants song.

It also helped Ken and Jerad's relationship. Jerad felt so guilty about the accident happening on his watch. Jerad had babysat the boys all summer long as a summer job for us. He was a responsible young man and very good with the twins. Ken did an awesome job as a father reaching out to Jerad and expressing his appreciation for turning off the lawn mower blades, and letting him know it could have happened to any of us.

On October 5, the boys were ring bearers for our niece Lacy's wedding. Despite the burn doctor's comment on our very first visit, "Oh, he's a twin. Well, I guess you will always be able to tell them apart," in the wedding pictures his burn was barely noticeable less than two months after the accident. I had complete faith that God was going to heal Justin's face without ugly scarring. And He did.

On Monday, October 9, 2007, I received a phone call that no mother ever wants to receive. At the end of the line was Cassie. She had been in a car accident, and all three of the boys were with her. I could hear screaming and crying, and it was obvious that Cassie was really scared. I ran out the school doors and raced to my van. I began praying frantically, begging God to get me there and to protect my children.

I called Ken's work number, then his cell phone. No answer. I began crying and begging God to hold my kids until I got there. Ken called back before I got to the scene of the accident. I told him that Cassie had been in an accident with the boys and said I would call back as soon as I knew whether they needed to go to the hospital.

As I came up to the accident, the entire right side of Cassie's car was gone. Cassie had been turning and was broadsided by a pickup. I knew the police officer at the scene and rolled down my window. I said, "Jeff, these are all my kids! Where can I park?"

All of the kids were out of the car. Justin was crying, Austin was in complete shock, Cassie was moving between all of the boys, and Jerad was bleeding badly from his face, neck, and legs. Jerad's eye was bleeding profusely and was being washed out with water by an EMT who happened to be at that corner (an everyday angel placed at the right place at the right time). The ambulances had not yet arrived.

Jerad kept saying, "Mom, stop crying! I am okay. Can I play football tomorrow? It's the last game. Can I play tomorrow? Are the twins okay? Is Cassie okay? Can I play football tomorrow?"

I went from kid to kid, talking to Ken on the phone, telling him about the kids and the vehicles involved. While they were checking the kids, the EMTs began cutting off the kids' clothes to check their wounds more carefully. Justin was put on a backboard with a neck brace, Austin had one little cut on his forehead, Cassie was bloody, but Jerad by far had taken the worst of it. I told Ken what hospital to meet us at, and that they were transporting all of the kids.

Three ambulances transported the kids. A close friend, Troy, drove my van behind the ambulances. This time they let me ride with Justin because he was complaining of chest and neck pains and wouldn't stop crying. Austin rode in the van with Troy, which we found out later, was a no-no. Through circumstances at school, I had gotten to personally know both police officers who helped at the scene, and they were wonderful.

"I will love You, O Lord, my strength. The Lord is my rock, and my fortress and my deliverer; my God, my strength, in whom I will trust; my shield and the horn of my salvation, my stronghold. I will call upon the Lord, who is worthy to be praised; so shall I be saved from my enemies" (Psalm 18:1–2 NKJV).

As I was trying to comfort Justin, I was praying and telling God how much I trusted Him, but I couldn't understand why this had to happen. I asked Him to give me strength for my children and for my husband. I thanked God for not taking my children away from us. I prayed for their complete recovery.

Praise the Lord; only a few hours later and with no serious injuries, all the children went home with Ken and me. Jerad had a ton of glass dug out of his face and hair, and he had to have several stitches on his face and both legs. Just like he had done at the scene of the accident, Jerad tried to talk the doctor into allowing him to play his last football game the next day, but for some reason, they denied him permission. In fact, the doctor said to Jerad, "If you intend to play tomorrow, I'll just wait to stitch you up because you will only tear all of them out."

Ken and Jerad looked at each other and asked, "Is that an option?" Silly boys! Jerad never lost his sense of humor, and God gave him extraordinary courage and strength.

All X-rays of Justin came back without showing any damage to his back, neck, or chest. Jerad and Justin had been on the right side of the car, and it was only through the grace of God that we did not lose both of them. This was Justin's second close call in less than three months. God must have an awesome plan for these boys. I can hardly wait to see how He is going to use them to further His kingdom.

Cassie was extremely shook up but basically walked away from the accident with only scratches and bruises. At the hospital, Austin finally began talking again. He had only one cut on his forehead. Thankfully, Cassie had made all of the boys put on their seatbelts before leaving the elementary school.

We serve an awesome and wonderful God. Within the next twenty-four hours, God showed me several reasons for this accident. He also showed His inexpressible love and lavished it upon all of us, but especially Jerad. Later that evening, Jerad asked me to sit with him and talk. He looked at me and said, "Mom, this accident was for me." I immediately interrupted him with protests, but he said, "Mom, just listen for a minute and let me explain."

He began to share from his heart. I stated earlier that we had been at my niece's wedding the weekend before. The entire weekend Jerad had been a real pain in the rear, a true teenager with attitude about everything. Both Ken and I had to have several talks with him, and Jerad was in the doghouse with his dad most of the weekend.

Jerad went on to say that he had gotten really mad at God for not helping him out. He said he even told God that he didn't know if he believed in Him because whenever he needed help, God wasn't there for him. Jerad then said, "Mom, God is real! When I was riding in the ambulance, God said to me, 'Jerad, you should never have walked away from this car accident. I am right here, and I love you.'"

Once again I was crying, because I knew God had used this accident to strengthen Jerad's faith. Every morning on the way to school, Jerad and

I talked about how much God loved him, and I encouraged him to look for God's working in his life. I smiled and said, "Jerad, God cares about every detail in your life."

Before the car accident, Cassie had stopped at the bank to allow Jerad to cash his babysitting checks. Jerad had a hundred dollars in his wallet, which was lying on the seat of the car. Some friends of ours were following the car as it was being towed and saw something that looked like a wallet fly out the side of the car. They were on their way to the hospital to bring clothes to the kids and decided they would stop and look on the way home. They didn't know for sure how badly the kids were hurt, and they were in a hurry to get to us.

On the way home, they stopped and found the money and some papers lying scattered on the ground, as well as Jerad's wallet in the ditch. The papers were gospel tracts that Jerad carried in his wallet to witness to other people. All one hundred dollars was in plain sight on the ground, and the tracts were lying directly on top of the money. No one had stopped to take it, and God gave back to Jerad everything that was in the wallet.

What kind of love does God show to those who love the Lord? Extravagant, undeserving, compassionate, detail-oriented love! God can use anything, good or bad, to daily reveal His unfailing love right before our eyes. God wants us to show this kind of love to our family, our friends, our acquaintances, and even our enemies.

In my conversation with Jerad the night of the accident, he expressed in detail his feelings of complete peace, a voice telling him numerous times that he was going to be okay, and being totally relaxed at impact during the accident. He remembered even chuckling and being completely surprised that there wasn't more pain. He also remembered being fearful for only a moment because he couldn't see and thought he had lost his vision. Not until he was actually in the ambulance did he realize how much he hurt.

The year 2007 finally came to an end, and I thought I never wanted to relive that year again. However, in January, Jerad had to have another surgery on his face. As his skin was healing, glass from the accident was rising to the surface, and some of it was coming dangerously close to his eyes. This was only the first of several opportunities to trust God during 2008.

The second incident happened a couple of months later. Ken and I were in the house when we suddenly heard bloodcurdling screams from the side of the house. I was coming from the laundry room and Ken was in the kitchen. Austin was running up the back stairs, crying, and Justin was right behind him, crying just as hard. Austin was covered in blood and was bleeding profusely from several places on his face. Justin was crying because he was so upset that Austin was hurt.

Thankfully, Ken was completely calm and picked Austin up and put him down on the kitchen counter while I located a clean washcloth to start cleaning the blood from his face so we could try to assess what had happened. Jerad came running in from outside and informed us that the neighbor's dog had bitten Austin. Cassie was frantic, Jerad was angry, Justin was sobbing, and Austin was staring at all the blood on his hands.

Through tears, Austin told us that he had been petting the dog when it turned around and bit his face. Austin pushed the dog in the chest to try to get him to let go. The dog did let go, but bit him a second time before he was able to get away from the dog. The first bite was above the eye and into his cheek. The second bite took a chunk out of his chin, and his upper lip and lower lip were just hanging. He had two gaping holes on his face: one hole was in the middle of his right cheek, and the other hole went through the skin in the chin area. His right eyebrow was missing, but praise the Lord, there was no injury to the eye.

Once again we headed to an emergency room. We stopped at the closest hospital. They took one look at Austin's face and said, "You need a plastic surgeon. You need to go to Children's Hospital." They told us that they would call ahead for us.

I was holding Austin in the backseat, and as we were traveling to the second hospital, Austin looked up at me and said, "Mommy, is the doctor going to be able to fix me?"

My heart was breaking, but I managed to respond. "Of course he will," I said. "Let's pray and ask Jesus to help the surgeon."

We waited for several hours in the Children's Hospital emergency room. The surgeon finally arrived and assessed Austin's injuries. At approximately 10:30 p.m., they asked us to leave the operating area. At the time, I was sitting beside Austin and holding his hand. I kissed him on the forehead and told him that I was going to pray and ask Jesus to help the doctor and to hold Austin's hand during the surgery since Mommy had to leave.

He smiled groggily and said, "Okay, Mommy. I love you."

When Ken and I finally got to the waiting room, I could no longer hold back the tears. I couldn't stop crying, and Ken just put his arms around me. I prayed for God to steady the surgeon's hands. We were told that he was the best plastic surgeon in Omaha, but I didn't feel like it would hurt to pray for God's help.

The doctor emerged from the operating room about an hour and a half later. Austin was still under anesthesia, but the doctor said that everything went well. Austin's skin had been completely detached from his face. The surgeon sewed rows and rows of stitches inside Austin's mouth to reconnect his skin.

Ken asked, "How many stitches, do you think?"

The doctor, without missing a beat, said, "Oh, well over two hundred stitches just on the inside of his mouth."

At 2:30 a.m., we were finally headed back home. We were exhausted but grateful that the surgery went well. I was sitting by Austin in the backseat. He tapped my arm and said, "Mommy, I saw Him."

I could hardly understand him because his mouth was so swollen. I asked him to repeat what he said. He said, "I saw Him."

"Honey, who did you see?"

"Mommy, I saw Jesus."

"You saw Jesus?"

"Yeah, I saw Jesus. He was holding my hand, just like you said He would. And He was watching and helping the doctor."

Tears once again began to stream down my face. I squeezed his little arm and smiled.

God completely healed Austin's face. He caught the flu at the hospital that night and threw up for two days. Thankfully, he never tore any of the stitches loose, and he was a trooper through the whole ordeal. Today Austin has a Sylvester Stallone snarl-type scar in the corner of his right upper lip and a small scar in his right eyebrow.

First Corinthians 13:13 says, "And now abide faith, hope, love, these three; but the greatest of these is love" (NKJV). The love shown by God to my family and me will be my strength for many more trials and years to come. My desire to encourage others has led to the writing of this book. My yearning to serve God and love Him unconditionally has given me the audacity to step out in faith and believe in the vision that God has shown me for my life. I will proclaim the faithfulness of God and His extravagant love.

What kind of love does God show to those who trust Him? It's extravagant.

Chapter Eight

Career or Not a Career— That's the Question!

"Lord, grant that I may always desire more than I can accomplish" (Michelangelo).

I don't remember exactly when or where I originally read this quote, but I wrote it down in my prayer journal. As I have thought about this quote and reflected upon it over the years, I cannot help but think about the significance of this prayer. How powerful could this prayer be in each of our lives if we prayed it daily and meant it?

If we Christians prayed this prayer, we would be constantly striving to accomplish God's will without question. I think we would tirelessly serve all brothers and sisters in Christ. Our focus and energy would be to serve God extravagantly, no matter the call. We wouldn't look at difficult situations or uncertain circumstances with a fixed mind-set or say, "What's in it for me?" There would be no lazy, halfhearted, or lukewarm Christians.

I remember as a senior in high school I couldn't wait to get out of high school. I was not going to go to college. I wanted to get a job, get married, and maybe have a couple of kids (I wasn't too sure about the kids). My guidance counselor was also my bookkeeping teacher. I was one of seven seniors to take his class with a straight A average all four quarters, so he thought I should become an accountant. Me, an accountant?

Absolutely not! I had no desire to sit behind a desk and work with numbers. It became quite clear to me that my guidance counselor didn't know much about my personal interests or me.

In July 1984, I realized that I wanted more out of life than working as a waitress in a coffee shop. I had worked at the Cozy Inn Café for two and a half years and really enjoyed people, but I wanted more than that. I had hated school so much that I didn't even want to discuss with anyone the idea of going to college. However, that particular summer day, I came home from work and told my mom that I had been contemplating the idea of going to college to get a degree.

My mom asked several questions as well as listened carefully. By the time we finished talking, I had decided that I should pursue a teaching degree in the area of music. In my eyes, it was my only area of talent that I felt comfortable pursuing. All through high school, I had loved to perform and was very active in stage band, swing choir, select groups, choir, and band. I had also played the piano for church and Sunday school since the fifth grade, so it seemed like the most logical and best choice as a possible career.

The very next day while I was at work, my mom went to Kearney. She picked up financial aid papers, a college application, and made an orientation appointment for me at Kearney State College. I was shocked. My parents had never pushed me to go to school. In fact, I thought they had accepted my decision to not go to college quite well.

I remember saying, "Mom, I didn't think this was that important to you and Dad. You have never said anything about me choosing not to go to college."

My mom smiled and said, "That doesn't mean that we haven't been praying for you to change your mind and go. I know you. When you have your mind made up about something, there is no use in arguing with you.

So I just prayed that God would change your mind." To this day, I am and will always be grateful for my parents' support and for allowing me to make my own decision to go to school without pressure.

"But know that the LORD has set apart for Himself him who is godly; the LORD will hear when I call to Him" (Psalm 4:3 NKJV). Each of us has been set apart for a specific purpose. God says He will be with those who are godly and seek His face. If we call upon the Lord, He will hear our cry and show us His ways. He will show His obedient children favor and bless them.

Ken and I met in January of our senior year of college. Ken wanted to move north to Michigan upon graduation, and I thought I wanted to pursue a master's degree in performance at Arizona State. I was in several performance groups at Kearney State and had been selected for a lead role the previous semester in an operetta. I loved performing and was starting to think about pursuing a career as an opera singer. I was working three different part-time jobs and spending every spare moment practicing for my senior voice recital. Ken was working full-time and going to school full-time. He intended to pursue a career in business but also wanted to be near some great lakes. (My husband is an avid fisherman. If he could fish and get paid to do it, he would be in heaven on earth.)

Ken graduated in May of 1988 and was offered a management position at Morris Press Cookbooks in Kearney. I decided that I was going to join a rock band for the summer. This group needed a female singer, and I thought it would be a fun summer. However, I planned to come back and student teach in the fall. Ken and I agreed that we weren't going to see anyone else over the summer.

I hated the rock band—okay, I hated being away from Ken. After two weeks, I called Ken and told him this wasn't the life for me. He drove nine hours to pick me up in Casper, Wyoming. By the end of October, Ken and

I were engaged. We got married on April Fool's Day in 1989 and moved to Grand Island, Nebraska.

That fall I started teaching music in Wolbach, Nebraska. I taught K–12 vocal and 5–12 instrumental music. I was also the head volleyball coach, directed a musical at both the junior high and high school level, added early-morning marching band to my duties, and gave weekly private piano, voice, and instrumental lessons. Ken and I were working opposite hours during the week. He traveled for weeks at a time the first two years we were married, and I was working eighty hours a week. When we did see each other, it was after 11:00 p.m. during the week. We ate a *late* dinner together and played Mario Brothers on the PlayStation.

Because I was maybe a little too driven to win in volleyball, and maybe a little too honest in regards to athletic abilities and musical talent, and set some really high expectations for commitment to both of these programs, a few people thought I was pushing the kids too hard. Okay, Let me explain. After *only* my third week of teaching, I sent down slips (failure reports) to *all* of my band students for not practicing their instruments. At the open house, my superintendent had to come rescue me. I got to meet every parent that night. Thankfully, several parents took their children's instruments home with them that night, and students started to turn in practice sheets. What a rookie mistake. I should have used a better strategy of communicating my expectations for practice instead of scaring the parents with a failing grade in band within the first three weeks with a new teacher. (Teachers, there are definitely better ways to communicate high expectations for excellence. I think they all thought I was a little crazy at first!)

In December of my second year at Wolbach, I found out that I was pregnant with our daughter. Because of the daily drive to Wolbach and my desire to be perfect in everything, plus having bitten off more than I could chew and hardly ever seeing Ken, I wanted to look for a different job.

Career or Not a Career—That's the Question!

Ken and I got into a heated discussion when I told him that I didn't want to return to Wolbach. He was adamant that we couldn't afford for me not to teach at Wolbach that next year. I told Ken that I would work several part-time jobs if it meant that I didn't have to teach another year. I was upset and told Ken that I was going to pray that God would open his eyes for him to see that I shouldn't teach at Wolbach another year. That same Sunday night, in frustration I prayed and asked God to help Ken see my point and to help me know what to do.

Right after school dismissed on Monday afternoon, I was paged to take a phone call. It was Ken on the other side, and it was obvious that he was distraught about something. His company had decided to close the facility that he was managing in Grand Island. He had been offered another position with the company, but we were going to have to move. We discussed that we were going to have to sell the house and several other things. Before hanging up the phone, he asked me to come to the facility on my way home. They were making the announcement to everyone that night, and then the managers were going to go out together. I hung up the phone and started packing my bag to head for home. My mind was racing when it hit me—we were going to have to move. I wouldn't be able to come back here to school next year. Praise the Lord! He had heard my prayer.

When I arrived at the facility, the secretary at the front desk was crying. I felt bad because several people were going to have to look for another job. Ken had told his secretary to ask me to wait for him in the conference room. I mentally reminded myself that Ken was distraught about this news, so I needed to contain my relief. After waiting for a few minutes, Ken walked into the conference room. He shut the door and sat down across from me.

"God answered your prayer." (Silence) "He knew I was too stubborn to listen to you about leaving your job. God knew that closing this facility was the only way I was going to see that you needed to do something different."

I smiled. We both knew that God had intervened on my behalf.

Things fell into place. God sold our house in less than ten days. I applied for an instrumental music position at Wilber, Nebraska. It was a relief and a disappointment when the job was given to another teacher. I know this is contradictory but I had really liked the school at the interview, and Wilber wasn't that far from Lincoln. However, I wasn't sure that I wanted to teach instrumental music only. Two weeks later, the vocal position opened at the same school. I called the superintendent and told him that I would be interested in taking the vocal position. He offered me the job. Not only did God provide a new job, but also He provided one in my preferred area of teaching.

As I said earlier, I was pregnant with Cassie. Her due date was August 12, so I was a little concerned about taking the job and not being able to start at the beginning of the school year. God took care of that too. Cassie was born on July 18, and I started school on August 12. He also provided a wonderful day-care provider, Sandy, who became a dear friend and mentor. We lived in Wilber for seven years. To this day, Wilber is my husband's favorite place that we have lived.

Psalm 139:1–5 says, "O Lord, you have examined my heart and know everything about me.

You know when I sit down or stand up. You know my thoughts even when I'm far away.

You see me when I travel and when I rest at home. You know everything I do. You know what I am going to say even before I say it, Lord. You go before me and follow me. You place your hand of blessing on my head" (NLT).

Wilber holds great significance for me as a Christian. It was in Wilber that I came to the end of myself and truly found Jesus. I decided to visit a new church in Crete mostly because my friend Dawn had invited

Career or Not a Career—That's the Question!

me. In fact, she had invited me several times. She talked highly of the pastor and was very excited about how quickly Crete Berean Church was growing. Dawn and I were both pastors' kids growing up, and we had a lot in common. She was also my accompanist at school, so we worked very closely together.

I knew I was just going through the motions of attending church. I was going to church on Sundays because I had been raised to attend church as a child. However, I was not being spiritually challenged or fed at the time, so I agreed to visit the church with Dawn. What could it hurt?

The pastor's sermon was very convicting and spoke to my heart. I felt like I was the only one in the room and he was talking directly to me. More importantly, I was very uncomfortable during the message. I knew I wasn't living a dedicated Christian life. Growing up, my dad always said, "If your toes are being stepped on in church, that means your feet are in the aisle." Pastor Lehmen was stepping on my toes!

Dawn insisted on introducing me to Pastor Lehmen after the service. During our conversation, he asked if he could come visit me that week during one of my planning periods. I thought, *I know how to talk to preachers. I don't want to sound rude, and school seems like a safe place for a little chat.* I told him that would be great, and we set a date and time to meet.

That little chat changed my life. During our conversation, Pastor Lehmen started telling me a story about his daughter. His daughter had rejected following Christ in her early twenties. As he shared about her finally calling him to come home, the Holy Spirit said, *Angie, he is talking about you!* I was crying, and so was Pastor Lehmen. He wiped his eyes and said, "Angie, I don't know why I am telling you this story." I smiled through my tears and said, "But I do."

At the young age of seven, I had asked Jesus into my heart at summer camp. However, alone in my office that day, I got down on my knees and asked God to forgive me of my sins. I told Him I was all in. I was His, and I no longer intended to be a Sunday-only Christian. I gave God everything that day and committed myself to live a life worthy of His calling.

Have you ever wondered if God made a mistake in where He has called you to serve, to work, to be a parent, to live? I know I have questioned my career choices. As I stated earlier, I could not wait to graduate from high school. I know that I told people that once I graduated, I would never enter a school door again. This fall I will be starting my twenty-eighth year as an educator and my eighteenth year as an administrator.

I have come to realize over the years that God doesn't care if I am a music teacher, a principal, a mom, a wife, or even where I live. He wants my mind focused on Him. Truthfully, that's all He wants from each of us. In fact, over and over in Scripture, we are promised a life of peace *if* we are filled and living in the Holy Spirit.

Romans 8:6 says, "So letting your sinful nature control your mind leads to death. But letting the Spirit control your mind leads to life and peace" (NLT). Without the guidance of the Holy Spirit, our minds become cluttered with things that only lead to unrest, confusion, disappointment, stress, anxiety, and worry. But in Philippians 4:6–7 Paul tells us, "Be anxious for nothing, but in everything by prayer and supplication, with thanksgiving, let your requests be made known to God; and the peace of God, which surpasses all understanding, will guard your hearts and minds through Christ Jesus" (NKJV). Perfect peace can come only through Christ. He is the Prince of Peace.

To be effective as Christians, we must seek God's vision and purpose. "Trust in the LORD with all thine heart; and lean not unto thine own understanding. In all thy ways acknowledge him, and he shall direct thy paths" (Proverbs 3:5–6 KJV). Ironically, God wants us to seek wisdom and understanding, but we are not supposed to rely on our own wisdom. God wants to have a close friendship with us, a walking-side-by-side-and-talking-daily type of relationship. In fact, I think we should walk so closely to God and know His voice so well that if He were chewing gum, we would know the kind of gum He was chewing and its flavor. My personal prayer has become, "Lord, let my desire to serve You be greater than anything I can accomplish on my own."

It is important to realize that God shares only portions of His overall plan with us. I believe He reveals specific details *when* we are ready to see and hear what He has prepared for us to do. I think that if He showed us everything at once and how it fit into His overall grand scheme for our lives, we would be too overwhelmed to be completely obedient.

The "aha" moment that comes, when you realize how God has used several different situations to mold you and prepare you for a particular circumstance, is incredible. As I look back over some of the most difficult trials that I have faced, I am amazed at how God has grown me into a confident woman who desires to have more of Him daily. That desire to know Him better has come from some of the ugliest moments in my life. God truly uses both good and bad situations to get our attention.

As mothers, as wives, as leaders at work, or as members of our church families, we must look beyond anything that we can accomplish on our own accord. Without godly wisdom, even good ideas won't necessarily be what God has planned for us to do. A fault of most women, myself included, is that we believe we must be self-sufficient. If we aren't able to check off items on our to- do lists, we feel we didn't accomplish enough for the day.

God doesn't necessarily want us running around doing everything that is good. Let's be clear—busyness and the fast-paced lifestyle of most

Americans are not God's ideas; they are men's. God wants us to focus on doing the best and most excellent things He has planned for our lives. To know the difference between the "good" things in life and the "best" things requires time alone with God. We must learn to hear His voice and distinguish the difference between what God is calling us to do and what the world thinks we should do. For many, many years I have struggled with saying no whenever I am approached about doing something for a good cause. And believe it or not, as a high school principal with a servant's heart, I still struggle not to try to solve everyone's problems.

"Do not let them [God's words] depart from your eyes; keep them in the midst of your heart" (Proverbs 4:21 NKJV). I need to spend time in God's Word daily. All Christians need to spend time in the Word. It is important to meditate on Scripture so that we can soak up truth and learn how to apply God's Word to our lives. Sometimes I read a verse in the morning and am not sure why it is significant; but it jumps out at me, so I pray about it. When I reread the same verse later that day, it suddenly makes sense. God often gives me guidance through His Word that prepares me for a decision that I am going to face that day. However, the truth is I don't always see the application until it's time to make the decision.

Proverbs 1:5 says, "A wise man will hear and increase learning, and a man of understanding will attain wise counsel" (NKJV). I believe that God has asked me to serve in the public schools. I also believe that I am called to serve as an administrator to encourage others to increase their learning and to build relationships with hurting people. Unfortunately, many times I deal with people who are not seeking godly wisdom or wise counsel.

Our society encourages leaders to influence people to follow them no matter what it takes. I often encounter people who rely on their abilities to manipulate, bully, or even use physical strength to influence others. In a cutthroat society, this type of behavior is often accepted. Sometimes ruthless leaders are even recognized as the ones who get the job done.

In June of 2008, I believe that God gave me a commission. Psalm 82:3–5 says, "Defend the poor and fatherless; do justice to the afflicted and needy. Deliver the poor and needy; free them from the hand of the wicked. They do not know, nor do they understand; they walk about in darkness; all the foundations of the earth are unstable" (NKJV). Also, Proverbs 31:8–9 says, "Speak up for those who cannot speak for themselves; defend the rights of all those who have nothing. Speak up and judge fairly, and defend the rights of the poor and needy." As adults, I believe we are called to stand up for those who cannot stand up for themselves.

To me, God was saying, *Angie, it is your job to protect all the children from ridicule, from despair, and from lack of justice. You are to stand in the gap and train others to care for the children lovingly and with self-control. Not all people understand that children are My most precious gifts to society. Give them hope for the future.*

To train people in the way they should go, sometimes as leaders we have to walk with them. In Judges 4, Deborah told Barak that God had commanded him to go into battle to protect the children of Israel. Barak was afraid and asked Deborah to go with him. "And Barak said to her, 'If you will go with me, than I will go; but if you will not go with me, I will not go!'" (Judges 4:8 NKJV).

Deborah agreed to go into battle with him. God delivered Sisera and his army into the Israelites' hands. Deborah didn't faint when adversity raised its ugly head. She asked God to go into the battle with them and followed His lead. The neat thing about this story is that God delivered Sisera into the hands of the Israelites in an unexpected way. In verse 9, Deborah agreed to go with Barak, but she shared this information: "So she said, 'I will surely go with you; nevertheless there will be no glory for you in the journey you are taking, for the Lord will sell Sisera into the hand of a woman'" (NKJV).

Sisera ran from the battle. He was on the run for his life from the Israelite army. He ran to the tent of Heber to hide from the army. Jael, Heber's wife, agreed to hide Sisera from the Israelites. Sisera asked for a drink of water, but Jael gave him warm milk to drink instead. She then covered him with skins and hid him at his request. Sisera fell asleep, and the story then took an interesting twist.

"Then Jael, Heber's wife, took a tent peg and took a hammer in her hand, and went softly to him and drove the peg into his temple, and it went down into the ground; for he was fast asleep and wary. So he died. And then, as Barak pursued Sisera, Jael came out to meet him and said to him, 'Come, I will show you the man whom you seek.' And when he went into her tent, there lay Sisera, dead with the peg in his temple" (Judges 4:21–22 NKJV).

You may be asking, "Angie how does this story relate to your commission?" To care for children, I am often required to speak on their behalf to their parents, to a teacher, or even to a coach. In today's society, many of our children have difficulty in respectfully expressing their needs to an adult. I believe that God has strategically placed me in my position of leadership to teach, rebuke, correct, and train in righteousness young people as well as educators. My job should be to equip students and adults with the tools they need to be successful in school, in their homes, and in their communities. Deborah was willing to go to war with Barak for the Israelites. I am called to fight for the souls of children in the public education arena.

Sometimes the battle seems impossible. Psalm 118 is a powerful psalm that has often encouraged me in times of adversity. There are several verses that have stood out to me: "The Lord is on my side; I will not fear. What can man do to me? . . . It is better to trust in the LORD than to put confidence in man. . . . The LORD is my strength and my song, and He has become my salvation. . . . This is the day that the LORD has made; we will rejoice and be glad in it" (verses 6, 8, 14, 24 NKJV).

In other words, it's not our battle—it is God's. God desires to lead praying leaders who are obedient to His Word so that He can use them at their workplaces, in their homes, in their churches, and in their communities. Psalm 56:9 states, "When I cry out to You, then my enemies will turn back; this I know because God is for me" (NKJV). In the past couple of months, God has once again answered many questions for me, and I feel the promise of future grace and peace in serving as an administrator.

Isaiah 37:35 says, "For I [God] will defend this city [school] to save it for My own sake and for My servant David's [Angie's] sake." For God's sake, I have been called to defend the fatherless and to speak for those who can't speak for themselves in our schools.

A career or not a career? Being a stay-at-home mom (or dad) to raise your children to know the Lord is a full-time job. No matter who you are, where you are planted, or what your occupation is, God loves you. God wants us to do what we enjoy doing. Our job as Christians is to share the gospel boldly in our homes, in our workplaces, and in our communities. We need to be full-time disciples. How we make our living is optional.

Chapter Nine

G.R.O.W.T.H. 16

"If you faint in the day of adversity, your strength is small" (Proverbs 24:10 NKJV).

This proverb has been a part of my signature at the bottom of my professional e-mails for the past five years. It serves as a reminder to me that I can always rely on God's strength. I added it to my e-mail signature to subtly encourage all people I communicate with in the digital world. Our strength is small only when we have not learned to rely on God's strength. My experience has been that God's strength is often revealed to me when I feel the most helpless, not in control, or at my weakest.

I love the book of Proverbs. King Solomon's nuggets of wisdom have been part of my daily morning reading for over fifteen years. There are thirty-one chapters in Proverbs. As I stated in an earlier chapter, for several years I have read a chapter a day to coincide with the day of the month. In months that have only thirty days, I read chapters 30 and 31 on the last day of that month. Each day I pick one verse from the chapter, write it down in my journal, pray about its significance for me that day, and try to meditate on it throughout the day.

When Cassie and Jerad were small, we often read the book of Proverbs together. They would listen as I read to them, and at the end of the chapter, I would ask them to share the verse that they liked from that chapter. We would discuss each of their verses, as well as the one I liked, and before bedtime prayers, all three of us would write down our special verse in our individual journals.

This is a practice that I intend to start with Austin and Justin this summer. In the past, I have read the New Testament with the boys and most of the Old Testament a chapter at a time, along with several age-appropriate devotional books. I think now that they are teenagers it's time to help them start to apply Proverbs to their daily lives. If this is not something you have tried, I highly recommend it. It is one of the practices that really started to bring the Bible to life for me as well as for my children.

At my current position, I spend a large amount of time working with seniors. About three years ago, one of my students asked me if I had a favorite quote. I had gotten to know this young lady quite well because for the last three months of school, I picked her up almost every morning on my way to school. I rattled off several different verses from Proverbs and ended with, "But I guess my favorite would have to be, 'If you faint in the day of adversity, your strength is small.'"

She asked two questions: "What does it mean?" and "Why do you like it?" It opened up an opportunity to share my faith and why I constantly read Proverbs. She asked me to write a few of the verses down for her, so I did, and didn't think that much about it.

On her last day as a student in high school, this young woman walked into my office. She gave me a pen-colored art project with the words of this proverb crafted beautifully in calligraphy in the center of it. She hugged me and thanked me for everything I had done for her that year and for helping her graduate. She then told me that she chose this proverb because I had said it was my favorite, and she, too, liked it the best from the proverbs I had shared with her earlier that year. I have this gift hanging in my office as a reminder to take advantage of every open door to share the love of Christ and God's Word.

As an educator, I love Christmas break because that is one time when I can spend a chunk of time reflecting upon my journaling from the entire year. I look back over scriptures that I have written down during my daily devotions, my thoughts and applications of God's Word, and prayers that God has answered. It helps me to recall the blessings that God has bestowed upon my family and me, as well as to remember the trials that God has carried me through that year. It has taught me to have an attitude of gratitude, as I have often cried when I remembered the sweetness of the Holy Spirit's presence during difficult situations and circumstances.

Can one word, a short phrase, or a verse become a part of who you are? I think it can. Let me share why I believe this to be true. During Christmas break at the end of 2008, I decided to develop a personal theme for the upcoming year. While working with students, I have learned that the use of visual reminders seems to have more impact in changing behavior than verbal instructions said over and over. I decided to write this theme at the top of my planner each day: "M.G.B.09" (Make God Big in 2009).

On January 3, 2009, I turned in a resignation letter without having another job. In early October, my superintendent had asked to meet with me in his office. He stated that he didn't think we were on the same page as leaders, and that our leadership styles were too different. I agreed with his statement completely. I realized during that conversation that God was releasing me. I had a sense of peace that I can't even describe. I knew my work at Conestoga was almost complete, so the first day back in January, I gave my boss my letter of resignation and told my staff that I would be leaving at the end of the school year.

I knew that God had given me a commission. I thought it was for the school where I was currently serving. Honestly, the start of the school year in 2008 was the best start we had experienced as a staff at the high school in the five years I had been there. In my opinion and the team of teachers that I had as advisors all thought the 2008–09 school year was a going great. However, for six months I had no idea as to where I would be serving God in the fall. Throughout those six months, people often asked me, "Where are you going to be next year?" My response was, "Only the Lord knows at this point."

At graduation, which was also my daughter's high school graduation, I was still answering that same question with "Only the Lord knows." At that point, I had been called for only one interview and had received numerous rejection letters. I was beginning to think that God was moving me out of education. But every day I wrote "M.G.B.09" at the top of my planner and told God that I trusted Him with my career and my family.

In the last week of school, I was called to interview at five different schools all within two days. All of the job opportunities meant that we would have to leave our home at Beaver Lake, but four of the schools would move us closer to Ken's parents. God's direction and His provision throughout the whole process were life changing for me. I left that school district on great terms with my superintendent. We met my last contract day, and he thanked me for finishing the school year with the integrity of a true leader.

God took care of every detail. I learned what it meant to truly wait on the Lord, to trust in His timing, and to experience unrealized blessings. Jerad got the opportunity to go from starting as a freshman on a football team that went 0-8 to playing in the state championship game on a team that went 13-0 in his sophomore year. He was even on the front page of the *Omaha World Herald* as he received his medal from his head coach. Later he went on to realize his dream of playing and starting on a college football team.

Psalm 82:3–5 says, "Defend the poor and fatherless; do justice to the afflicted and needy. Deliver the poor and needy; free them from the hand of the wicked. They do not know, nor do they understand; they walk about in darkness; all the foundations of the earth are unstable" (NKJV). Since 2009, I have continued to pray for a theme for each year. Each year the theme has held great significance as to things that I experience during that year. In 2010, it was "20T.M.10" (The Mission). In my first semester, I started praying every day during my twenty-five-minute drive to school, and I cried and prayed almost every night driving home. God showed me then and continues to show me why He has given me a commission to serve the poor, the fatherless, the afflicted, and the needy.

My theme for the year 2011 was "20LWF11" (Live Without Fear). Less than a month after I started writing this theme at the top of my planner, an assistant principal at Millard South was killed by one of her students. This incident reminded me that I shouldn't waste even one moment of my life. I started to pray for God to open more doors to share the gospel and to give me the boldness to speak truth.

Acts 9:26–27 says, "And when Saul had come to Jerusalem, he tried to join the disciples; but they were all afraid of him, and did not believe that he was a disciple. But Barnabas took him and brought him to the apostles. And he declared to them how he had seen the Lord on the road, and that He had spoken to him, and how he had preached boldly at Damascus in the name of Jesus" (NKJV).

Barnabas went out on a limb for Saul (Paul) early in his ministry. He believed that Paul was going to be an asset to the disciples and apostles in spreading the good news of Jesus Christ. The Scriptures tell us they were afraid of him and basically thought Paul was a fake. Praise the Lord for Barnabas's courage and insight to encourage the early followers of Christ to embrace and support Paul in his ministry. Paul became one of the most influential leaders in his time. Plus, look at all the Scripture he wrote that helps us today.

Throughout the Bible, Barnabas is known as an encourager. His willingness to invest in others is also demonstrated in the following passage concerning John Mark: "Now Barnabas was determined to take with them John called Mark. . . . Then the contention became so sharp that they parted from one another. And so Barnabas took Mark and sailed to Cyprus" (Acts 15:37, 39 NKJV). Paul and Barnabas were divided over John Mark. Barnabas obviously could see Mark's potential to grow and help in the spreading of the gospel, but Paul apparently wasn't impressed with Mark's leadership skills at the time. They were so divided that Barnabas took Mark to Cyprus, and Paul asked Silas to join him on his mission trip.

I find this ironic because Barnabas was the one who had taken Paul to the apostles because they didn't believe in him. Barnabas must have been blessed with discernment and the ability to see true character in the rough. Both Paul and Mark were used greatly by God to further His kingdom. A side note to this story: When Paul was imprisoned in Rome, he wrote to Barnabas, asking him to come to him and to bring John Mark along. He believed that both of them could help him in Rome. Paul showed his true character and was able to admit he had been wrong about Mark. He asked for him by name when writing to Barnabas.

At Administrator Days in 2011, we were challenged by one of the motivational speakers to have "one word" for our purpose and mission for our schools. This was reaffirming to the things that God had already been showing me. Prior to Administrator Days, I had suggested that we develop a school theme using one word for our upcoming school year. We had already established our word. At every session, I listened to see how many times people brought up our word in their talks. Believe it or not, in every session I attended, the word was used numerous times in different contexts—*focus*.

Taking this concept further, we were challenged to find a word for ourselves as a theme for the upcoming school year. God automatically brought the word *invest* to me. I wrote the following to remind myself to constantly look for opportunities to invest in others that year:

> INVEST: I am to *invest* in students, teachers, colleagues, and parents to ensure that all students receive the best-focused education possible. I am to *invest* in the students that no one else can reach. I am to *invest* time in my own family and their lives. (Jerad was a senior that year, and I didn't want to miss anything important during his last year in our home.)

I also decided to use *focus* as part of my yearly theme for January of 2012. Each year since, I have tried to incorporate my personal theme with our advisement theme at school. This reminds me that I have a call to serve God not only in my home, but also at work.

2012: 20-F.O.C.U.S.-12 (Focus On Christ Understanding Sacrifice)
2013: 20-B.+F.-13=Be C.R.O.S.S.~F.I.T. (Christ Reigns Over Self-Sacrificing Servants~Focused Intentional Training)
2014: P.R.E.S.S. 14 (Pray and Rejoice Earnestly Seek Sanctuary)
2015: G.R.I.T. 15 (God Reigns In Trials)

My current theme is G.R.O.W.T.H. 16 (God Requires Ongoing Water-Walking Towards Holiness). This year has been a year for me to really grow as a Christian. I have finally realized that if I want to walk on the water with Jesus and experience His power, I have to get out of the boat.

I started this book in 2003. It was written and edited for several years. I have been talking about getting it published for over ten years. In July 2015, God challenged me to put my e-mail devotionals on Facebook, and in May, He prompted me to contact a publisher. I thought it was completely ready to send in, but I couldn't seem to end the final chapter. I prayed about how to end chapter 8, and God told me I had one more chapter to write. Selecting a yearly theme has greatly impacted my walk with Christ, and I needed to share this concept with all who would read this book.

I know this is the first book of many to come. God has reminded me that I need to *invest* time into writing. He has commissioned me to encourage, to bless, and to lead others to a life focused on Christ. If you haven't made a decision to follow Jesus, do it now! He will answer your prayer for help.

"This is 9-1-1—may I help you?"